Collective

Callum Bell

Panswed

First published by Panswed in 2024

© 2024 Callum Bell

Typeset in Sabon Next LT and Gill Sans Nova

Callum Bell has asserted his right under the Copyright, Design and
Patents Act 1988 to be identified as the Author of this Work

British Library CIP Data available

ISBN: 978-1-0686984-0-8

Printed and bound in Great Britain by
Imprint Digital Limited, Exeter, UK.

For Amy

nā 'sato vidyate bhāvo
nā 'bhāvo vidyate satah

'The unreal never is; the real never is not'
The Bhagavad Gita II (16)

Table of Contents

Introduction

This book has been in my head for a number of years. There were various catalysts. One was watching an Adam Curtis documentary entitled *The Century of The Self*. Curtis ended the documentary with a question – how do we follow the (twentieth) century of Freudian individualism and neo-liberal capitalism? The answer soon became clear to me: with Jung and the collective unconscious. I had long been interested in the things that molecular biologist Rupert Sheldrake had to say about this and related topics. Indeed, my previous attendance at several events where he had outlined his thought processes is testament to the fact. Around this time, I found myself in the audience at a talk delivered by the philosopher Mary Midgley. Her passionate refutation of reductive science helped to cement my view that a less materialist conception of the world might be the correct one. It felt as though a response to Curtis might be based on similar ideas. Throughout this period, I found myself collecting philosophical ideas that were useful to this end, one of the other important ones being Bernardo Kastrup's analytic idealism.

It is one thing to accumulate ideas which suggest that reality might be a little more to do with spirit or – to use contemporary language – consciousness. It is another thing entirely to understand that the nature of such consciousness may be collective; in other words, it is shared and universal. The ideas which I find so inspiring also have it that humans are unaware of this shared aspect, hence: *collective unconscious*. Finally, it is something else again to conclude from this that the majority of our everyday communication is of a different, degraded nature to this collective communion. The argument which I will attempt to construct in the following pages, includes the suggestion that our quotidian social interaction often serves to *disrupt* this theorised higher and unconscious shared mentation. Themes of this nature are developed, and a conclusion emerges: it is that the goal of our lives is to learn how to move beyond the everyday noise, because it is ultimately of little benefit. Furthermore, noise – or if you like, distractions – are increasing in the age of the digital paradigm. We now consume ephemera from the moment we rise to the moment we fall asleep. In the lyrical words of Ray Bradbury in his masterpiece *Farenheit 451*, 'we are eating shadows for breakfast'.

I believe that the arguments for a non-material basis of reality are convincing. Some of these are purely philosophical (see for example, the works of Bernardo Kastrup). Others find evidence in the persistence of folk wisdom regarding the unity of things. They recur in a variety of cultures and epochs, and some are remarkably similar to Jung's own descriptions of the collective unconscious. However, my interests are broader than theories and analysis set down on the page. I have learned a great deal from the direct experience: music, raves, unconventional and Afro-diasporic social events. These form a central part of this book. As Fela Kuti once opined (Kuti, 1988), Africa has its own knowledge to offer the world. While I am very enamoured with European philosophy, I nevertheless believe that it is time that the world weaned itself away from a culturally hierarchical attitude to knowledge. Africa, I think, opens many new and useful pathways to the collective unconscious. If only the world were able to embrace African modes on an equal footing, we might perhaps learn new things, and forget other notions which need to be discarded.

While sat outside my tent at the *Tonnau* music festival in North Wales on a sunny weekend in September of 2021, I began to sketch the outline of this text. It was a book I was very excited to write. Primarily, I wished to complete it for myself – to organise the ideas about reality that I had been pondering for well over a year. I also felt that a text such as this one might be useful for other readers. Perhaps it is an attempt to offer hope, or simply to create an alternative mental model through which to frame twenty-first century life. Of course, I have no idea if this book will be a palpable or *pulpable* success (as my friend Professor Helena Flam once inadvertently punned). Nevertheless, if you read it with an open mind, you may find yourself intrigued by the concepts within.

In all of this, my role is conduit. I certainly am not the great thinker – those whom I reference in this volume fall into that category. Therefore, if what you read arouses your interest, I urge you seek out the sources. Read Sheldrake, read Kastrup, read Jung. Read Sonya Richmond, Juan Mascaró, and the Vedantic texts. Study Han, McLuhan, and Debord. If you do this, and also begin to import these alternative mental schemata into your everyday patterns of living, then my hope is that together we might begin to break the rules of modern life and generate a mode of existing which is new and different and hopefully better.

Collective

Paradigms

The idea that there is an enigmatic collective force which connects us is a pervasive one. It is a theme which has recurred in philosophies, theologies, and folk wisdom across the span of human existence. The *collective* (which is the term I shall employ as a shorthand throughout this text) is a reference to the notion that human beings and in some cases, all living things, are connected in a non-physical way. Many of these philosophies describe a mysterious psychological unity in the form of impersonal shared mental stuff. It has variously been referred to by the psychologist Carl Jung as the *collective unconscious*, by the philosopher Bernardo Kastrup via his term *transpersonal mentation*, and as *Brahman* in ancient Indian philosophy (although Brahman is much more than an impersonal entity in this tradition). In addition to the concept being central to the psychology of Jung, the analytic idealism of Kastrup, and the *Vedantic* texts of India, similar ideas can be found at the heart of other cultures. These include the Rastafarian notion of *I and I*, the Amerindian/Mexica *universal consciousness* which Kuauhtli Vasquez describes, the *one spirit* of the Australian Aborigines and the African concept of *Ubuntu*. If one listens closely, references to the idea of a non-physical, impersonal unity can even be detected in some elements of contemporary popular music.

In early twenty-first century western societies, living what is considered a good life is a demanding business. The majority of any population are unlikely to give a great deal of thought to constructs such as the collective unconscious, unless they are involved in academia, spiritual groups, or religions. Most would probably assume that an unconscious collective is a fantastical or at best, high-minded notion which concerns only philosophers, poets, and preachers. This book is an attempt to convince readers that not only might this enigmatic collective be real, it may also be one of the most important aspects of a life (in fact *the* most). The reference here is to the psychological, non-physical aspects of life, and not the material domain, which contemporary western society tends to focus on. The material and the non-physical are of course intertwined. Even so, the lived experience – the joy, sadness and pain which ultimately determine the quality of a life are all psychological if not spiritual. Nevertheless, I am fully aware that a sizeable segment of readers will be sceptical. The collective which I am referring to, is merely a concept; it is intangible and disputable. Ideas such as these are easy to dismiss, largely because our everyday concerns are shaped by an aggressively materialist world view, which we are assured is the only way of framing the world. This narrative includes the practice of science, and the way in which its findings are shared. Indeed, the social structures of the scientific community reinforce the materialist worldview to the exclusion of competing philosophies. On top of this there is our popular culture – the media, work, fashion – all of which bolster the notion that everything is material, and we are isolated individuals within a reality of physical stuff.

It is easy to test the idea that our beliefs are defined by the prevailing discourse. Who amongst us has seen an electron or a quark? The scientists who understand these particles inform society of their existence and describe their properties. Our social environment encourages us to (or rather, demands that we) respect the work and the conclusions of the scientific community. Therefore, on the whole, we accept the pronouncements of these women and men without question. Note, that I am not questioning the existence of electrons or quarks, I am simply demonstrating that society generally outsources the construction of knowledge to this community. It is a wonderful arrangement when the conclusions are correct, but a little more troublesome when the scientific paradigm finds itself up a blind alley – which happens more frequently than many might think. Nevertheless, our acceptance of scientific knowledge is usually helped by the practical application of the science. For example, understanding the behaviour of atoms and electrons gives us electronics. As a music lover, the hi-fi equipment and sound systems which reproduce my favourite recordings, are a valued application of this knowledge. And of course, the entire edifice of internetworked digital technology, which powers much of the contemporary world, is another such end-product.

In the nineteen-sixties, the physicist turned philosopher of science, Thomas Kuhn published a book entitled *The Structure of Scientific Revolutions*. In it he attempted to describe the way in which science progresses. Rather surprisingly, his conclusion was that science is not guided by raw, objective evidence alone. Kuhn proposed that science advances via *paradigms* – these are rigid scientific world views based on conclusions confirmed through previous studies. Importantly however, a paradigm also manifests as social agreements in the scientific community, for example, regarding the subjects which are valid for study and those which are not. Kuhn provided historical examples of the way in which evidence that challenges a paradigm may be initially disparaged as 'experimenter error' or similar, until the weight of anomalous findings causes the entire edifice to collapse. Eventually, a new paradigm will replace the old one. Viewed from the perspective of Kuhn's historical analyses, it can be surmised that all paradigms ultimately collapse. Indeed, the other inference is that even the science of today will be subject to challenge and replacement. I like to characterise Kuhn's theory of paradigms as the conflict between the raw empirical observation versus the theory which scientists create to explain any phenomenon. The following are examples of this.

In times gone by, the earth was considered to be flat. The ancients did not just dream up this idea, it was based upon sensory observation. If one looks to the horizon one can clearly see the apparently flat nature of the landscape. However, following improved observation, technological advancements (for example, ocean-going boats) and more creative theorising, it was determined that the flat nature of Earth was an illusion. On a large enough sphere, the view to the horizon appears level to the observer. Another useful example is the conflicting ideas about the position of the Earth in the heavens. As is well known, the Greek mathematician Ptolemy (100 AD–170 AD) placed the Earth at the centre of the universe. Again, this was based upon the observations of the senses. If one looks to the sky, the sun, stars, and planets appear to circle the Earth. There is something narcissistic about our sense of self: the ego, the I, seems to be the datum of everything out there. Hence, it is unsurprising that our planet occupied this position within Ptolemaic astronomy. Once again, with the passage of time this was later demonstrated to be naïve. Advancements in observation and calculation led to a new theory that the Earth was not central, but rather was just another orb, itself circling the sun. The new cosmology took a little while to get used to, but when it did, the Copernican era was born.

These *paradigm shifts* are not limited to scientific advances in the ancient period alone. The formulations of Sir Isaac Newton led to many of the material technologies which we take for granted today (certainly in the west). In the period following Newton, artists and philosophers were compelled to bow to the practical power of his materialistic cause-and-effect conclusions. The advancements in science and engineering proved the worth of the paradigm. Nevertheless, the cycle of shifts continued, for even Newton and his classical physics were subject to replacement.

Throughout this period, observations had been noted which appeared to contradict a number of the central understandings of classical physics. As per Thomas Kuhn's description of paradigms, these anomalies were flagged as experimenter error or considered invalid for other reasons. Eventually, a brilliant scientist named Albert Einstein was able to incorporate the oddities into a new paradigm. Special and general relativity explained all that Newtonianism could, but also that which the old science could not. Thus, in hindsight, classical physics was shown to be comparatively naïve in the same way as Ptolemy was in respect of Copernicus. Finally, the arrival of quantum mechanics, two decades or so on from special relativity, was the final nail in the coffin of classical physics.

In our contemporary era, there is a rich and complex science which explains the phenomena that surrounds us and importantly, also allows the development of stunningly useful technologies. It is a science which enables the sending of spacecraft to Mars, or the creation of computer applications that can instantly translate one language to another. We can determine the position of a handheld device anywhere on the planet to an accuracy measured in centimetres and supply real time directions to another location. It is easy then, like those eighteenth and nineteenth-century artists and philosophers, to prostrate ourselves before this science, and accept its greatness, for its ends have proven its veracity. Nevertheless, the same might have been said of the (subsequently superseded) classical physics. If science had ceased pushing boundaries, had given up on the attempts at falsification, and if humankind had not (eventually) dismantled that successful paradigm then the apex of the achievements of our species would have been Victoriana: the engine, bridges and building technologies; sanitation. It is important to recognise that electronics, computing, advanced cosmology, and space travel was only possible once the Newtonian paradigm had been overthrown.

Our current science, based on quantum mechanics, relativity, and other great theories in biology appear to the lay person to be unassailable. However, at the fringes of the academies are individuals who are engaged in the old tradition of challenging the status quo. Many of their perspectives emerge from the failure of the current paradigm to deal with the subject of consciousness: what is consciousness? Did it evolve? How does material science explain that which seems immaterial? This is a huge subject area on which many thousands of words have been published, and it would be better to point you towards them instead of attempting my own rehearsal here. Nonetheless, I would ask that you simply keep the following in mind. Science is based upon observation, and while the conclusions drawn from observation may appear plausible, history has demonstrated that in hindsight, the observations may be deceptive and the conclusions naïve. Worse yet, when a paradigm is in play, science is rarely humble enough to realise its destiny; that is, the fate of all theories and paradigms. They will be superseded by something else.

To return this to the subject of this text – the collective – contemporary lines of scientific reasoning would conclude that such notions are unproven. The social agreement born out of paradigmatic orthodoxy would go further: subjects such as this are not valid for study. Terms including *pseudo-science* would be likely to feature in any response. Within the walls of the materialist academies the matter would end there. However, although the topic of the collective is extra paradigmatic and generally excluded from the academies, it is still of interest to many deep thinkers. Amongst their number may be those who will be the catalyst for the fracturing of the current paradigm. Besides, ideas about the connections between humans is the everyday, lived stuff of spirit or psyche. If the collective as Jung and others describe it exists (and I believe it does), then it exists regardless of the current scientific reasoning. The deep experiential existence of even modern-day homo sapiens runs somewhat apart from the cold antiseptic science which attempts to be the authority on such matters. Imagine a situation in which scientists were to request that you prove that you are in love during a marriage ceremony. 'Detail your proofs!' they might insist and point to a specially prepared blackboard in the registry office where you would be expected to outline the material and mathematical rationale for your relationship. The point is that not everything is as reductive as the current paradigm would suggest.

Collective

This treatise concerns the reality that we are surrounded by, but not the material reality which is the focus of contemporary science. It is the reality of you: of consciousness, mind, and soul. It is the reality of us – living things. There are some on the fringes of the academies who are attempting to construct a new paradigm. They argue that the reality of consciousness is in fact the *greater* reality. In other words, that the material world is *an effect* of immaterial consciousness. These debates are intricate and as much as I would like to rehearse them here, I suspect that this would be folly. It is better instead I think, to direct you to one of the leading exponents of this idea (which is known as *analytic idealism*), Bernardo Kastrup. In his book *Why Materialism Is Baloney* published in 2014, he patiently deconstructs the materialism which is taken for granted at the present time, and outlines a plausible, parsimonious, and consciousness-based alternative. We will return to Kastrup later. What of the collective? It is a hazy concept and is something which has been hinted at by both ancient and contemporary thinkers. The existence of such a phenomenon has not been nailed down in the way that modern materialist science demands. However, for our purposes, proofs are not a pre-requisite. In our lives we never have to prove that we are in love, or are happy, or are depressed. These are *experiential* states, which are a little removed from materialist science. If we accept these emotions from the perspective of our own internal experiences, then we should not find it difficult to also add the idea of the collective to such an experiential category and explore it from a non-physicalist perspective.

There will be some readers who will only feel comfortable with the orthodox forms of materialistic and reductive science. I fear that I may be in danger of losing some of you at this point. Nevertheless, I would like to passionately attempt to encourage you to stay. I too am enamoured of science, physics, and technology. Furthermore, my entire career has been in the field of computer science, which is probably as practical an application of physics as exists at the present time. However, I can simultaneously explore the notion that there may be something else; like love, like consciousness, like lived experience. These are at least as real as particles and materials (and perhaps not reducible to such). It is not either/or. Those who remain reading are hopefully at least open to exploring novel hypotheses related to these notions. I am in good company. The previously mentioned philosopher Bernardo Kastrup is also a computer scientist.

I am sympathetic to the view that ideas which persist over millennia have some form of basis in truth. For example, the concept of an afterlife is one that features in numerous epochs and cultures. We find references to post-mortal psychic persistence both in ancient Sanskrit societies (circa 500 B.C.), as well as present-day near-death experience research. Modern-day information technology enables the collection and storage of information, and partly because of this, it is now understood that near death experiences (NDEs) are a relatively common experience. Those who survive death events are greater in number than ever before due to advances in medical procedures, such as resuscitation, as is detailed in Sam Parnia's 2014 paper *Death and consciousness*. From such research we are led to the conclusion that in the past, individuals will have also (if less frequently) reported the experiences that today are well documented in the NDE literature. It is therefore unsurprising that the belief in an afterlife has remained a constant throughout human history; even persisting through the fervent materialism of the recent past.

The collective is another persistent idea. This, as with the concept of the afterlife, is also encountered in ancient Indian Vedantic literature. *The Bhagavad Gita*, a key text in this tradition, contains numerous references to the unity of things. The ancient Greeks also subscribed to the idea of a non-physical collective. Marshall McLuhan – who we shall also hear more of in due course – suggested in his 1967 text that 'what the Greeks meant by "poetry" was radically different from what we mean by poetry. Their "poetic" expression was a product of a collective psyche and mind' (*The Medium is the Massage*, p. 113). Carl Gustav Jung, who along with Sigmund Freud was one of the pioneers of psychotherapy, held the collective unconscious as a central concept in his psychological theories. According to Jung, there is an element of our psyche which is shared. This is not directly accessible, but it influences our functioning. For example:

> The unconscious is the psyche that does not govern perception and muscular activity like the cerebrospinal system ... but ... it maintains the balance of life and, through the mysterious paths of sympathetic excitation, not only gives us knowledge of the innermost life of other beings, but also has an inner effect on them. *In this sense it is an extremely collective system* (*The Archetypes of the Collective Unconscious*, p. 19 – emphasis mine).

Many are familiar with the Freudian personal unconscious: thoughts, memories, and feelings, which are beneath the threshold of recall, but nevertheless exert an influence on our motivations and desires. The collective unconscious of Jung is similar except that the memories and feelings, which are contained therein, are not necessarily personal. They may be related to our familial, cultural, or even species past. That is, they are unconscious echoes of the experiences of those who are related to us in some way.

The concepts described by Jung have been developed by a contemporary biologist named Rupert Sheldrake (see for example his volume *The Presence of the Past*). His theory of *morphic resonance* expands upon Jung's quite difficult, and sometimes vague concepts. According to Sheldrake, the reason that an acorn grows into an oak tree is because it accesses a species memory which influences the shape and attributes that the young plant must adopt. Memory at both the individual and collective level is shaped by habits – cumulative consequences of our past behaviour. The collective growth habits of the oak family *are* the collective memory of the species. Sheldrake applies morphic resonance then, to explain inheritance of physical and psychological characteristics, including instincts. It may surprise readers to learn that biology does not have firm understandings of the processes by which such outcomes occur. Genes are usually offered as the explanation, but as Sheldrake points out, while genes play an essential role in the organisation of fields of cells, they do not explain the organisation itself. Hypotheses such as morphic resonance, which seek to fill the gaps in the explanatory scope of contemporary science, may ultimately lead to a brand-new paradigm; one which is quite different to the materialism that currently informs knowledge.

If the inferences of Sheldrake and Jung are applied to sociological issues, one begins to understand ways in which a new paradigm might shape future discourse. I, for example, am a member of the African diaspora. My parents emigrated from the Caribbean during the Windrush era. My family are therefore the descendants of African slaves. Applying Sheldrake's morphic resonance to this scenario, the four-hundred year back catalogue of suffering in my ancestral line might bear an influence on the collective habits and memory of the cultural group with whom I share this history. Attitudes and behaviour within particular communities are of great interest to sociologists and might be understood more clearly with reference to theories of the collective unconscious.

The persistence of the idea of the collective can perhaps be used as evidence for this overall hypothesis (in much the same way that persistent ideas of an afterlife might be explained by near death experiences). But what if we were one day able to determine beyond reasonable doubt, the existence of such a collective. How would this knowledge affect the way that we live? It is difficult for even the most brilliant thinkers in this area to claim to understand how such a collective may operate – its causes and effects, and what it may mean for ontology and epistemology. The fact is that regardless of the science and philosophy that will be presented in the following pages, this subject – and more specifically, this book – can be considered to be something like the equivalent of a book about love. No scientific proofs are required, just an open-mindedness towards the phenomenon in question (even if it is not understood) and a willingness to explore the ways in which it absolutely and definitely influences our lives.

In addition to writing about the collective, I will also explore the notion that there is such a thing as a *false* collective. If that shared memory hinted at by Jung, Sheldrake, and others involves communing on an unconscious level, then one might conclude that it serves a purpose. One such purpose may be the biological inheritance that is described by *morphic resonance*. It may also be something else, yet to be ascertained. Whatever the purpose, or purposes are, they will have been a feature of life on earth throughout the various stages of evolution. Indeed, the importance of the collective unconscious might surpass mere inheritance. It may in fact be the basis of what it is to be alive. I commune; therefore I exist. The difference between organic metabolising material and silicon computers, for example. Thus, to return to the writings of poets, sages, and thinkers through the ages, we should perhaps note their exhortations to live in harmony with the collective. If to commune is to live, then the more we commune, the better our quality of life. In contemporary society, sentiments such as these are rarely expressed in the mainstream of science and academia. In this volume, the ideas about how such communing is best achieved are taken from other texts which detail this: the ancient Vedantic philosophies, existentialism, the works of Byung-Chul Han, and Guy Debord. The reason for invoking the topic of the false collective is to suggest that if the processes of the collective exist, they are subtle and easily ignored. More importantly however, they are also subject to disruption by other social activity in a culture. The disruption is of the nature of communication over material channels – at the current time I particularly have in mind digital activity. This *false* collective may be of a different quality entirely to the communication that takes place in the psychic, enigmatic, and immaterial collective. It is more immediate, accessible and we are told it is all there is. This is why the former obscures the functioning of the latter.

Made From Love

A number of ideas have been introduced which will be expanded upon in the pages that follow. The natural starting point is, of course, the collective. There are various historical and cultural perspectives on this. I shall start gently, with the pervasive folk wisdom which is expressed via phrases such as 'we are one' or 'all things are connected'. Often, the 'we' in such statements refers to the local social grouping or perhaps even humanity as whole. In some instances, it encapsulates the entirety of life. Amerindian (see for example, Kuauhtli Vasquez) and Aboriginal cultures are good examples of this. Folk wisdom of this nature is encountered in even more diverse communities, including the one I grew up around, Rastafarianism. Rastafarians describe their fellows using the term 'I and I'. This is used to signify the unity between the subject person and the object person. Here we find a strong inference of the collective. How did Rastafarianism develop this notion? It may have been imported from other cultures – the Amerindian natives of the Caribbean who originally inhabited the islands perhaps, or even the Indian workers brought in by the British in the nineteenth century. I am open to the possibility that this idea may have been divined via the effects of marijuana which is consumed in large quantities at Rastafarian ceremonies (similar to the way in which metaphysical insights are often reported by users of psychedelic drugs). Either way, a deep connection between community members has been recognised as a truth by this social group and this perceived unity is a central tenet of their belief system. Moreover, true Rastafarianism is associated with vegetarianism and even veganism (via the eating of *Ital* foods), reflecting a concern with the well-being of all life on the planet.

Rastafarianism is probably best known in relation to the music of Jamaica. Reggae grew out of the movement from the nineteen sixties onwards, and many of the early recordings within the genre were laced with Rasta ideals. I grew up towards the end of the *roots reggae* period, surrounded by the music. It was quite something to be part of a youth sub-culture which had at its heart deeply spiritual tenets. Peers of mine were members of other musical tribes for example, punk, soul, or funk. I enjoyed being exposed to the different genres and flitted in and out of various groups. However, it was always pleasant to retreat back into the deep culture of reggae – even if it also involved parties at which we danced until dawn, drinking, and attempting to make it with girls. Nevertheless,

Rastafarianism was the serious philosophy which ran in parallel with the youthful carousing. Robert Nesta Marley (or plain old Bob to much of the world) played a major role in popularising reggae in the west. As this music increased its reach, the ideas of Rastafarianism infused the mainstream. It is certainly not unusual to attend a music festival these days and encounter a reggae legend on stage intoning Rastafari scriptures to a receptive audience. These formerly obscure doctrines were once only heard by the relatively small number of those in the Caribbean diaspora. Now Rastafarian messages are global. The young people who are listening to reggae today are being introduced to a particular form of the philosophy of the collective via this medium.

If there is even the possibility that such a thing as a mysterious, unconscious collective actually exists, then perhaps it behoves us to try to fathom – from our experience, from the writings of others, and from our own reasoning – what it might mean for our lives. In Indian Vedantic philosophy, we read that humankind is part of a universal omniscient whole. A similar realisation is often reported during near death experiences. These, admittedly subjective, reports have proliferated in recent times (see for instance, Pim van Lommel's paper published in *The Lancet* in 2001). Online, one can read numerous examples of those who sensed the unity of all things while in the near-death state. Furthermore, Rupert Sheldrake has studied phenomena that he argues are related to his theory of *morphic resonance*. These include what might be termed telepathic incidents – the sense of being stared at, or pets seemingly knowing in advance that their owners will soon arrive home. He suggests that these episodes may be indicative of a collective unconscious through which such mysterious forms of information transfer may occur. Using current materialist science to ascertain the answers to puzzling phenomena of this nature may be problematic. As I stated at the outset, science as currently practised, is an excellent method for uncovering the causal relationships upon which our physical world rests. However, as with the superseded historical theories mentioned earlier, the conclusions arrived at from contemporary empirical and observational methods may be correct in a particular context, but they may subsequently prove to be naïve. In the end we may require a quite different philosophical lens through which to understand the whole.

The collective of Rupert Sheldrake concerns relations: that is, familial and ancestral groupings. It extends even beyond this however, to the implicit connection between members of a species. His *morphic resonance* theory suggests a collective cognition; a memory which is distributed amongst living entities which share a bond. The more powerful the relation, the stronger the sharing. Therefore, the young of genus *giraffa* will develop species-defining characteristics such as the long neck and legs, horn-like ossicones, and distinctive coat patterns not via genetics per se, but rather through access to the memory of the shape into which to grow. Any instinctive behaviour that creatures exhibit is, according to this theory, also the result of the contents of the species collective. Furthermore, this hypothesis posits that *new* collective memories can be acquired and shared in relatively short time frames. For example, Sheldrake published the results of an experiment in which male mice were taught to be fearful of a specific chemical. This was achieved by administering an electric shock to the mice at the same time as their being exposed to the substance. Sperm from these mice were used to inseminate females artificially (the females and males never physically encountered each other). The resulting children and grandchildren of these mice froze with fear upon encountering the chemical (see Rupert Sheldrake's 1992 paper entitled *An experimental test of the hypothesis of formative causation*).

The collective of morphic resonance then, is based upon relation. What is relation? Sheldrake is a biologist therefore his understandings will be based upon reproduction and genetics. This is obviously not the case with some of the other conceptions of the collective already mentioned. For example, the philosophy of the Vedanta takes an attitude mirrored in Socrates' statement that love is the messenger between the gods and man. The carrier wave of their collective is love. Not romantic love alone (although that is a subcategory of the love they describe), rather a deep affinity and empathy with other things. Platonic love, we might call it. The practical philosophy of Yoga stresses that humans should cultivate such feelings until it becomes a habit to think of others in such a way. It is, the unknown sages argue, through these methods that one can fully realise one's humanity and place in the cosmos.

How then might the relation of Sheldrake sit with the love that is at the centre of Indian philosophy. I am reminded of a lyric in a recording made by Stevie Wonder in the mid-nineteen seventies. The song *Isn't She Lovely* was written as a celebration of the birth of his daughter. In fact, the artist objected to the release of the record, but his protestation fell upon the deaf ears of the management of Motown records (the episode ultimately proved to be the catalyst for Wonder to part company with the label, but that is another story). The song contains the lyric 'Isn't she lovely, made from love'. With these words, Wonder implies that human reproduction is the product of love. Here then, we find the link between Sheldrake and India, via Stevie Wonder. Sheldrake's relation is a relation of love; love via familial ties, or species ties. It is often easy to forget that families are nominally formed through a union of genetically unrelated individuals (either via marriage, co-habiting, or sexual relations). These unions are, as Stevie might put it, made from love. They spawn subsequent generations; the future. The sages may have nailed it – perhaps love is the key.

In the nineteen nineties I was a psychology undergraduate student at the University of Sussex in Brighton. It was a formative period both personally and intellectually. The proscribed reading in the cognitive psychology module introduced me to the concept of *the self*. It was a fairly respectable subject area at the time, and I read a number of papers written by a key researcher, Hazel Markus. This nineteen-nineties idea of the self was, I think, a precursor to the contemporary idea of consciousness. The research seemed to almost broach the topic of consciousness but couldn't quite cross a particular (and probably paradigmatic) line. It is interesting to note then that the seeds of the current brouhaha surrounding consciousness were planted at the same time that I was reading about the self in the University of Sussex library. This is because the paper that kicked it all off was *Facing up to the problem of consciousness* which was written by David Chalmers and published in 1995. However, in the earlier studies of the self, its central role in human cognitive functioning was posited. For example, empirical research suggested that memory recall is enhanced for concepts related to the self. For example, *my* wife, *my* brother, *my* car. This effect holds true even for concepts which are related to others who are linked to the subject self: my wife's car, my brother's house, my friend's clothes (see Markus & Sentis, 1982). The self is that which one knows best. It is the datum 'I' which we have the strongest relation to. In other words (and apologies for the oblique reference to another soul music record), the greatest love of all is for the 'I' within. Entities which are most closely related to that 'I' (and remember 'relation' was earlier equated to 'love') are evaluated in a similar manner to the 'I'. This network of relation is easily visualised via what is known as a *social graph* (and here my background in informatics is very useful).

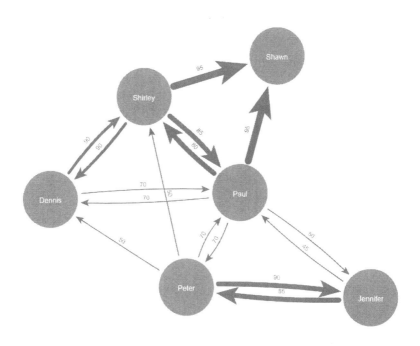

Figure 1. Social graph featuring Paul and his relations (created using Neo4J Aura)

The circles are *actors* (persons or other entities). They are sometimes referred to as *nodes*. The lines are *relationships* which illustrate directional connections between nodes. The line width in this instance indicates the type of relationship (wide = *parental*, medium = *romantic*, thin = *sibling*, thinnest = *friendship*), while the numbers represent the strength of the connection. Regarding the illustration above, let us put ourselves in the shoes of Paul. This chart is a diagram of his self-relations. We can see the strength of the parent-son relation between Paul and Shawn (95), the romantic paring between Paul and Shawn's mother Shirley (80/85) and also the friendship bond between Paul and Peter (70). These will themselves be stronger than the friendship between Paul and Jennifer (50) which is as a result of the strong romantic pairing of Peter and Jennifer (90).

The phenomena reported by Hazel Markus and others whereby closely-bonded individuals are evaluated similarly to oneself may – in language that Rupert Sheldrake might employ – be a morphic resonance effect between related parties. These relations then, may not be genetic and/or proximal as contemporary understandings would have it. Indeed, if we substitute the word *love* for the dry psychological term *relation*, it sheds a slightly different light on the connections between us. Western societies tend to obfuscate love relationships; that is, it puts them into a box. It assumes that they only exist within very specific romantic and familial contexts, and also *in extremis*, between a small number of close friends. The theories of Sheldrake and Jung, however, suggest that we have unconscious collective relations with a greater number of others, both alive and deceased. We can have love relationships with the departed of course – parents, spouses and children who have passed away for example. A number of the various theories of the collective suggest there is an even greater network of ties – inter-species relations with pets for example (see Sheldrake & Smart 1998). Moreover, expansive relations with members of our own species may be the conduit by which we connect to unconscious ancestral memories. Obviously, we are unaware of these, hence unconscious. As with the mice in the Sheldrake experiment, such memories may influence the future form and behaviour of related organisms. Thus, morphic resonance would suggest that a son may grow to resemble a father because of the strong relationship between the two; the memory – or habit – of the shape into which to grow was shared. However, if we overlay morphic resonance with the ideas of Jung especially, we would need also to conclude that the same boy will also share memories with other, more removed members of homo sapiens, for example on the other side of the globe. This is because for Jung, the contents of the collective memory can reveal themselves as archetypes which are common to members of a species. A lesser effect perhaps, but still a result of relations – in this case between members of genus *homo sapiens*.

If these theories accurately reflect the reality of things, then they describe a collective communing, and it implies we influence one another without necessarily being aware of the fact. Furthermore, the channels through which this operates are obviously not yet understood. Perhaps the task of clarifying the processes of the collective is one for future science – or perhaps it is not. The scientific method, which has been so successful in its particular domain, may only yield stunning applications in the world of material. The domain of consciousness is, at least at present, largely one which is philosophical and spiritual. Contemporary psychology (which is very different to the work of Freud and Jung) has hitched its wagon firmly to materialist ways of conceiving the world. For many years the discipline appeared to suffer from a chronic envy of the successes of the physical sciences and so eventually, it threw its lot in with them. Neuroscience dominates the discipline today. Thankfully, philosophy enables us to engage in discussion of subjects such as consciousness and the collective in language which does not necessitate appeals to materialism. Are the most meaningful discussions about music conducted in terms of frequencies, amplitudes, and time intervals? Do we consider the actual experience of being in love primarily from the perspective of brain chemistry? It would be a strange world indeed where young people expressed their amour in chemical formulae and proofs instead of love poems.

We have thus far lightly meditated upon hints of the existence of the collective and their apparent persistence over time and across cultures. The preceding text has introduced various hypotheses about the possible nature of the collective. One such conception is that expounded by the philosopher Bernardo Kastrup. He reasons that the connection between us arises from the fact of all metabolising matter (that is, living things) being part of a universal mind; the All. The idea is even more profound than at first appearance when one understands that Kastrup, an *analytic idealist*, considers that the true reality behind the phenomenological appearance of things is consciousness. Not *your* consciousness or *my* consciousness, rather this universal mind. He believes that we are all separated *alters* within the whole. At the edge of me, which borders the edge of you, is what Kastrup terms a *dissociative boundary*. We are made of the same stuff; that is, of the universal consciousness, but the boundaries fence us off and cause us to appear different to one another. Kastrup and this entire topic are wholly fascinating and if this has piqued your interest, I wholeheartedly urge you to explore his writings and videos in detail.

The analytic idealism of Kastrup also mirrors some of the ideas in Vedantic thought. Is the similarity of these notions co-incidence, co-influence, or are they an echo of a universal truth? We find the idea of the collective in (for example) the culture of the Greeks, Amerindians, Aborigines, and the Rastafarians; in Sheldrake, Kastrup, and Jung. The same concept is present in the philosophy of the ancient Indians, and in reports of NDE experiencers and psychonauts. Of course, almost certainly there will be instances where thinking will have been influenced by predecessors. For instance, we can see clear lineage from Jung to Sheldrake and Kastrup. Furthermore, there are those who suggest that ancient Greek thought was influenced by the older philosophy of India. However, the determination of the answer to this question is not the point of this essay. It is enough to acknowledge that these ideas have persisted. The recurrence of this concept across cultures and time will, I hope, cause readers to pause to weigh my arguments for the existence of the collective.

Let us take the hint of the notion's persistence then and assume that we are all connected. It might be because we are made of the same stuff; part of a whole with only a boundary that dissociates us from others. Our connections to each other can alternately be imagined as something like an enormous version of the social graph in figure 1. In this latter imagining of the collective, it becomes clear that some links are stronger (family, friends) and others weaker (culture, species), but connection there is. Applied to our real lives, it might be that when we experience a sense of connection, relation or – in the language that I prefer – love, this can be described in terms of the collective. Depending on the model that you choose, we are either activating the links that bind us, or dissolving the boundaries which separate us.

The Kastrup model of dissociated alters is powerful, but it doesn't explain why certain pairs or groups feel more of a sense of connection than others. If the notions of Sheldrake, Jung, and of course the Vedantic sages are employed, they allow us to posit that the answer is love. It is highly likely that Kastrup has considered this, but many of his writings are for scientific audiences for whom concepts such as love would not be very well received. The Vedantic writings stress that cultivating the feeling of love for others can engender what might be termed a mystical sense of oneness and well-being. I have been reading these ancient texts since my late teens and at times have practised the methods which are contained within them. From my personal experience, I can attest to the inner change that occurs. I find it easier to cultivate the mindset of connection or love for all in certain heightened emotional situations – when I feel in danger, for instance. Or at music festivals – and this is an area which I shall explore in much greater detail.

Whether through dissociated boundaries, relations, or oneness, such a shared consciousness (or more accurately *un*consciousness) might perhaps be responsible for the emotional reaction experienced when viewing abstract art, listening to music, or even reading. Perhaps when one human communicates with another, even via asynchronous media, part of the exchange takes place in the unconscious collective domain rather than the purely physical. Rupert Sheldrake criticised what is termed the *information processing model* of human consciousness. This has it that the mind is the brain, and it resembles a computer. That is, it contains a central processing unit, memory, and input/output interfaces. According to this model, the entire phenomenon of consciousness takes place via these internal modules. For instance, we hear sound via transducers (our ears), which convert the sound waves into signals, which our brain can process and transform into language. The trace of the aural event is then stored in our neuron-based memory. Sheldrake proposes an alternative understanding. He suggests that only a part of consciousness is local. The model he offers is one in which the brain is akin to a local radio transceiver which communicates with a larger remote device. This remote device is not exclusive to an individual but is shared and it is this which constitutes the collective. Our brains can both transmit to and receive from this larger remote mind, and he postulates that such a mechanism might underlie the processes of morphic resonance. The central collective memory will store, for example, the shape and characteristics of a giraffe. A newborn of that species can access this information, and this will determine the shape that it grows into, as well as the instinctual behaviour to exhibit.

Morphic resonance leads Sheldrake to investigations of phenomena which include telepathy and collective problem solving for example. These he integrates into notions of collective information processing. In an example of the above, he suggests that solving a day-old crossword is easier than solving a brand-new puzzle because the older one will have already been completed by perhaps millions of others, and the solutions will be available in the collective unconscious. If the maverick biologist is correct, it would not take a giant leap of conjecture to imagine how such processes might influence our everyday behaviour in ways that we are not aware of. If we also inject the Vedantic notion of love as a key process within the collective, then we might begin to build a new way of regarding ourselves; one which is radical for both the individual and for society. I intend to explore this in more detail in the following pages.

False Collective

In addition to exploring ideas about the collective, this essay is also concerned with another type of group consciousness, which I will term the *false collective*. The shared unconscious that I have described to this point is little understood but is theorised to be universal and perhaps (according to the Vedantic tradition and modern analytic idealists) is the basis of reality itself. The false collective is the material communication which dominates our lives in the early twenty-first century. This rather more prosaic commune might be described as the worldly social environment which brings us into proximity with each other, and also describes the content that we exchange via these physical interactions. In form, the false collective appears similar to the universal one, however, there are qualitative differences. For example, the links of the material collective can simply be grounded in proximity; the people whom we live close to, work with, and who are for example, schoolmates. Love is not a significant factor *per se* in the connections of the false collective. Note however, that simple relations such as these can be the catalyst for the development of deeper bonds in one's life. For example, a life partner might only have been initially known to the other because they live in the same community or attended the same school. Obviously, such a relationship might develop to the extent that it becomes grounded in love. This may subsequently lead to a new family and a proliferation of further deep connections. There is an interplay between the false collective and the deeper, affection-based one described earlier. We may initially be thrust together in a material sense, but from such mechanical interconnection may arise a web of relation that has a higher nature. Furthermore, when discussing proximal relations in our century particularly, it is important to note that proximity is not only physical, but also digital. A partner may become known to their significant other via online meeting places – Internet dating services and social media groups are two obvious examples.

The collective has its basis in processes unknown. The universal mind of Kastrup, the Brahman of Vedantic thought, or the collective unconscious of Jung are all ineffable to a greater or lesser extent. In some traditions, the collective, and our selves within it, are defined by love. The false collective may share some attributes with its universal namesake; however, these are deceptive. The two collectives are of entirely different natures. For example, one could create a social graph of a segment of a material community. This might appear to be very similar to a network of relations based on love; the social graph in figure 1 is a pertinent example. A key difference is that the false collective is loveless by default. Another important distinction is that physical networks can be managed or manipulated by humans and corporations. Media is an appropriate example, and social media even more so. We can be subtly encouraged to watch a particular movie, to frequent a specific venue or to 'love' a brand. The ends of such suggested activity are not rooted in an ineffable profundity of emotion; neither do they interact with the moral and spiritual well-being of an individual. In our material twenty-first century existence – and specifically under the dominant western economic philosophy of neo-liberal capitalism – the goal of the false collective is often profit and/or power for economic and political entities within society. We are often brought together to work (produce) or to buy (consume).

It is not always a simple task to differentiate between the two collectives. On the one hand, there is the universal, foundational collective of the Vedanta, Jung, Sheldrake, and the cultures referred to earlier. On the other, there is the *false* collective; the marshalling together of human beings – by chance sometimes, and for specific purposes at others. The digital sphere by its nature, would fall into the latter category. It is essentially artificial and the connections between the nodes of this network are largely manufactured (especially so in the present-day Internet). It is interesting that among some techno-futurists, the mass of human interaction on the Internet is sometimes termed the *hive mind*. This is an apparently emergent phenomenon created through billions of online conversations. If the Internet and social media were truly random then it might well have been possible to describe it as a technologically mediated reflection of the true collective. If this were the case, we might be able to say that the collective which emerges from the Internet is *technologically enhanced proximity* at best. However, today's Internet is intensely manipulated in order to engineer encounters and exposure to ideas. This means that chance events are not always what they seem. The reason of course is that much of the modern Internet is guided by algorithms which have as their end the increasing of particular outcomes for the platform owners and advertisers. The ideas that they wish users to be exposed to, and the encounters they seek to engineer are the ones that benefit them. Sometimes the desired outcomes are not always immediately capitalistic; for example, a valued result of a platform design might be *stickiness*, that is, the tendency of a service to keep users engaged and present. While not directly related to profit or other goals of capitalism, it is an indirect route to the desired ends. If a platform can attract millions of visitors, retain them, and ensure that they return frequently, then this platform will become popular with advertisers.

There is much to say about the false collective. It is, I think, the more difficult of the two collectives to describe. The universal collective has been a topic that has been examined by philosophers over millennia. The false collective is slippery, it evades definition. One is unsure whether to approach it from the perspective of sociology, economics, social psychology, or (of course) philosophy. The false collective is the water in which we swim. It is all-pervasive, and so to attempt to step outside of it, and to look back in for the purpose of analysis is no easy task. To understand it, we must embark on a journey without maps (perhaps we are guided by a few sketches on a grubby paper fragment). Happily, I am accompanied on this expedition by a number of scholars. Amongst them are Marshall McLuhan, Byung-Chul Han, and Guy Debord. Additionally, as in so many aspects of my life I am also aided by my love of music which often helps to illuminate ideas that I have become fixated with.

As I write this, I am sailing on the good ship *Cotentin*, a Brittany Ferries vessel which is crossing the English Channel between Le Havre and Portsmouth. I am returning from a vacation in southern France. While there, I spent some time listening to French pop radio stations and visited two local nightspots. I became aware that the relationship which mainstream French society has with popular music, appears somewhat different to that of countries with a more respected Afro-diasporic culture. This idea served as an interesting metaphor of the differences between the true and the false collective. Why is this? It is because western pop music is primarily Afro-diasporic music. The art-forms (for example, what became blues and jazz) were incubated by the displaced Africans during the slave trade of the sixteenth to nineteenth centuries. In the section of this volume entitled *Black Music as a Psychic Technology*, I hypothesise that this music was a *technology of consciousness* that helped the slaves to survive the brutalities to which they were subjected. The technology, I argue, works by allowing participants to access the true collective. The time spent in this universal consciousness freed those in bondage, at least temporarily, from the nightmare material existence which they inhabited.

Modern societies with a strong connection to the Afro-diasporic cultures in their midst implicitly respect this deeper function of the artform. Therefore, DJs such as Gilles Peterson (BBC Radio 6 Music) do not use the music solely as a vehicle for dance floor ego and vanity. Rather they employ it as that technology which enables the assembled revellers to access the collective in a spirit of love and unity. The French *boites de nuit*, which I visited these past two weeks, were seemingly devoid of this spirit. The events seemed to me to be focused upon material things: *beauté, vanité* and *égoïsme*. It seemed to me that this was their understanding of the purpose of disco, funk, and soul: all glamour and power, and less unity and collective striving. I feel certain that not all French nightspots operate in this manner. Indeed, the same Gilles Peterson was formerly the curator of an annual festival in Sète – a French town only a short drive from the region in which I spent my vacation. Moreover, there are utterly prosaic night clubs in the United Kingdom which operate on the same principles as the cheesy French nightspots that I had the misfortune to visit. Finally, a mention of the excellent French radio stations Nova and FIP demonstrate that in certain quarters there is an understanding of the deeper purpose of Afro-diasporic music on the other side of the English Channel.

The musical detour above illustrates, I hope, one of the difficulties of attempting to highlight the difference between the true and the false collective. If one regards surface appearances only, one can easily be misled into confusing the two notions. Even more important than the problems I face writing this text, such differentiation is a problem of life. It is necessary to make choices regarding the activities we wish to engage in, the people we wish to spend time with and the places we wish to visit. Some are more aligned with the universal, others with the unreal. I feel that there is an element of our make-up which draws us to the universal collective and its default mode: sharing love. When we engage in this way, we seem to be rewarded; our psychological well-being is enhanced. When distracted by the false collective however, we receive the short-term pleasurable chemical hits often described by neuroscientists. However, the longer-term psychic outcomes are not always as benign; these can include anxiety and a sense of worthlessness. Nevertheless, we are often confused as to which is the collective that we should engage with. Fortunately, I have arrived at a stage of my life where I often find myself asking – is this real? Is this unreal? And the answer guides my choices.

My current situation serves as a useful example. I am writing these words in a café in Sheffield. Everything about its appearance seems to indicate that this is an establishment which has aspirations that align with the collective. It is frequented by musicians and artists, its décor is natural, retro chic, and is located in an aesthetically pleasing neighbourhood. I am here because I have passed this place on many occasions and from the outside looking in, I always assumed that the atmosphere would be one in which the patrons reach towards that unconscious communing. However, until I am as sure as I can be about this, I remain open to the possibility that it may simply be a hipster, gentrified, and materialistic hangout for the cool people to enjoy.

The complexity of differentiation challenges us in all manner of social situations. In this I also include digital interactions. Society encourages us to fall in love with that associated with the false collective: things, brands, status. As suggested earlier, left to their own devices, most positively inclined human beings would default to seeking out environments where they can share love with other people. In contemporary western societies the accepted outlet for this instinct is either a romantic relationship or a family. Nevertheless, even in situations where this nuclear need has been satisfied, there can be a supplementary desire for a more expansive relational horizon. Our culture tends to obfuscate opportunities for true love and oneness beyond the family, erecting a smokescreen of entities that an individual may instead desire: wealth, power, and status. These are not always presented in their raw form of course. For example, the classy car is often a cipher for sex appeal which comes close to being a substitute for love but is probably more of a metaphor for power. The list of these diversionary tactics is, in fact, extensive. Beauty falls into this category, for example, in the form of social media-published images of wonderful experiences in glamorous locations. In fact, social media as well as regular advertising on television or other media encourages one to love these attributes of the unreal. Furthermore, the techniques involved in manufacturing these desires often employ the language and images of the collective, unity, and love. The irony is that the former are anathema to the latter, and here one begins to sense the shape – and the slippery nature – of the false collective.

Magic and Memory

If we were able to part the curtain of the false collective and peer beyond it, I think that we would immediately sense the possibilities for love and oneness that are still replete in the world. The Vedantic Yogis offer methods for doing this; one of the most compelling of these is that named *Karma Yoga*, which will be examined later in this text. These ancient psycho-spiritual practices require dedication and focus however, and the modern world of distraction makes it difficult to embark on such a path. A method which readily presents itself to the contemporary citizen (although one that offers only a temporary taster of what the Yogis describe) is the music festival. More will follow on this particular topic in subsequent pages, but for now, it is enough to quote artist Rachel Horne's description of music festivals as 'spaces which break the rules of modern life'. What this means in part is the temporary tearing down of the curtain of falsehoods and allowing (at least for a long weekend) revellers to move closer towards the oneness and love that is a feature of the true collective. Many who experience this effect at festivals are aware of the significance of it. They can subsequently find themselves at a loss as to how to recreate the openness of the festival experience in their everyday lives.

Interestingly enough, I am writing today in a café named *Kollective*. It is a peaceful space attached to the *Site Gallery* in the centre of Sheffield. There is something about art and music which I think is aligned with the true collective. I am always struck by how, at a concert, either the music or the words of an artist can have a unifying effect on an audience. I could list many examples from recent years, however, my experience at the Samm Henshaw performance at the *Love Supreme Festival* in 2022 will illustrate the point. His Sunday afternoon appearance on the main stage was an electrifying gig by any standards. The entire set seemed to be concerned with speaking to the inner self rather than any outward-facing ego. At the time, I had not previously encountered this artist, so I was especially blown away. One of the last songs that he performed was a number entitled *Joy*. As the song progressed towards its finale, Henshaw slipped into effortless improvisation. It was the first summer that festivals were permitted to take place after the COVID pandemic and within society, uncertainty about the future was still palpable. During his freestyle lyricism, the singer began to reflect this and attempted to reassure the audience by repeating the words 'everything is going to be alright'.

Finding his stride, and with the band locked firmly in the groove, he asked members of the audience to turn towards the person standing next to them and repeat the words 'everything is going to be alright'. The audience complied. It was magical. I complied. I looked at the woman next to me and she spoke the words with a surprising degree of sincerity, as did the thousands of people stood on the grassland in front of the main stage. This, in my view, was activity that was enacted beyond the curtain of falsehood. It invoked the true collective; a unity and (non-romantic) love.

The best visual art also seems to operate at the level of the collective unconscious. Jung alludes to this with his focus on archetypes and mandalas. Previously, I had never understood why I reacted strongly to particular artworks and the way in which they might operate on my psyche until relatively recently. For example, this summer I attended an exhibition of work by German contemporary artist, Neo Rauch. Taken at face value, and interpreted via everyday sense-making, his pieces are bizarre and even a little frightening. However, while regarding the works, I began to suspect that they were operating on the level of the unconscious. Not the Freudian personal unconscious – it is unlikely that the sea-mammal / human chimera, which is a feature of his paintings, relates to anything in my individual experience. However, I accepted the possibility that some collective thought or memory of cruelty, dominance and power might be at play. Other abstract art may similarly operate at the collective level.

As mentioned earlier, I am a member of the African diaspora, a citizen of the UK via Caribbean heritage. My parents were born in Grenada in the West Indies as were their parents and grandparents. The abolition of slavery in the British Empire was completed in 1845, therefore in the not-too-distant past my ancestors will have experienced slavery. This would be the case for all in my line stretching back through the hundreds of years following the forced emigration of some unfortunate forbears in Africa. Obviously, slavery was no walk in the park. It was long hours of work in hot, horrendous conditions. Death, all manner of pain, and a kaleidoscope of emotional anguish were but a few of the perils. In contemporary debates it is sometimes suggested that because transatlantic slavery is a historical event, the descendants should forget and move on. However, and this is the point of raising the topic of slavery here, should the ideas of Jung and Sheldrake hold any water, then the weight of that accumulated suffering; the unconscious backlog of it, will loom in the collective that the descendants of those slaves inhabit. Not only that, but the reverberation of those events may also reside in the transpersonal mentation of those who were the slavers. Without going into detail, I have particular archetypal thoughts that have been present since my youth and are concerned with authority and power. If I assess these in the light of the idea of both the collective unconscious, and my cultural history, only then do they make sense. I may be reacting to my history in a manner comparable to Sheldrake's mice.

Dreaming Ahead of Time

I have outlined the key elements of the collective, as well as its false counterpart. It now may be useful to introduce ways in which we may experience the shared unconscious ourselves. It is not always straightforward, however. For example, one result of such experiences is the considerable cognitive dissonance which is felt afterwards. This is because situations are encountered which would be difficult to make sense of when interpreted in the way that contemporary society demands - that is, via materialism. However, if one chooses to think beyond the physicalist orthodoxy then it may be possible to experience the collective oneself. Grasping such an understanding might help an individual to make sense of episodes which materialism struggles with. To repeat a point made at the outset, science is excellent for uncovering the cause-effect relationships in the material domain. However, the meta-layer of existence, described by the Vedantic philosophers and Bernardo Kastrup, is posited to be an extremely vibrant and highly experiential aspect of existence. In an ontology such as this, material reality is a sub-effect, a screen, a dashboard. It is Plato's famous 'shadows beyond the cave'. Behind this effect is a reality of pure consciousness.

I was recently introduced to Gary Lachman's recent book entitled *Dreaming Ahead of Time*. In chapter five of the volume, the topic of Jungian *synchronicity* is explored. Synchronicity is often confused with coincidence. However, the latter term refers to random events which are simply co-occurring in time. Synchronicity implies an additional element, *meaning*, and therefore synchronicity can be summarised as 'chance events with meaning'. An important aspect of the Jungian phenomenon is that the meaning referred to must be specific to the person that experiences it. Random co-occurrences which *lack* meaning are simply chance events. For example, if a person was having warm thoughts about a friend that they had not heard from for a long time, and that person suddenly called, that would be synchronicity. Thus, to experience synchronicity, one must be open to coincidental events which have significant meaning to oneself. It is not simply the events and the meaning themselves, but also our recognising the significance. It is only then that the depth of the phenomenon is realised. In Jungian terms, it is the conjunction of internal and external events which hint at an unseen and greater reality. Jung considered the phenomenon to be closely related to the concept of the collective unconscious, and archetypes. He also considered that the purpose of synchronous events was to warn, guide, or demonstrate universal truths to the recipient.

From a personal perspective, I recognise these events most often at music festivals. It may simply be that I am more open to synchronicities at these happenings due to features of the environment. For example, I enjoy dancing (note that I am a child of nineteen-eighties hipster London, therefore my preferred mode of dance is not the formal, rehearsed type, rather improvisational, nightclub moves). In favourable circumstances, I find that dancing in this way expresses something of spiritual importance. Two years ago, I found myself in such a surrounding: a large festival venue. The DJ – *Madame Electrifie* – was playing music which, to my mind at least, was having a positive effect on the entire audience. Apropos of nothing, a tall, shaggy-haired North American man suddenly approached me. 'Let me tell you about dance' he said. For the next twenty minutes, he proceeded to outline what I assumed was his personal philosophy of dance. He insisted that it was something to do with being 'open' and 'closed' simultaneously. I had smoked a small amount of marijuana and had drunk a few beers at this point, but what he said had significant meaning. While he spoke, I continued to dance and interpret his words with my movements. I wondered afterwards if he was under the influence of psychoactive substances (hardly unusual at a music festival!). Nevertheless, his approaching me and talking deeply about dance (which I take seriously) fit my description of a meaningful coincidence. It is one event of many that I chalk up as an example of Jungian synchronicity.

The kinder sceptics and materialists might designate the episode above as simple over-emotionalism on my part. I certainly sympathise with that perspective. During much of my earlier life my reactions to similar events have been along those lines. However, in truth there has also always been an underlying curiosity about alternative ways in which to frame existence. This reaction emanates from a part of myself that has not completely succumbed to the narrative of my education and the society in which I was raised. The Gary Lachman volume offers an interesting non-materialist perspective via his discussion of *pre-cognitive dreams.* Lachman posits that dreaming of events which are yet to occur, is a common phenomenon. Dreams of this nature he suggests, are not those which relate to significant incidents; rather they make reference to minor, everyday situations. At a talk that I attended at *How The Light Gets In* philosophy festival in the spring of 2023, he discussed various episodes of this nature. I was in the audience and afterwards was summarising the key arguments to a fellow attendee that I had become friendly with. She reacted sceptically initially, suggesting that the entire theory was outlandish. Surprisingly however, in the next breath she proceeded to describe a dream that she once had in which a lizard was seen in the middle of the road. The day after having the dream, her son called her to the window because there was a lizard in the road outside her house. I informed her that this was precisely the kind of dream to which Lachman was referring.

Lachman suggests that the frequency of these incidents is underestimated because the vast majority of dreams are immediately forgotten upon waking. In his talk, he challenged the audience to make a note of their dreams, and they too would experience the phenomenon of pre-cognitive dreaming. I decided to put this to the test. On my return, I resolved to note my dreams for a period of two weeks. However, on the second day I experienced my first pre-cognitive event. I dreamt about a situation and then later that day, in real life, I stopped at a local café. While drinking my americano, two other people at the next table were discussing a very similar situation using the language that I had heard in my dream. A day or two later I noted down another dream. In it, someone approached me and said excitedly 'Haven't you heard? The government has resigned'. My wife and I enjoy the drama of UK politics and neither of us is overly enthusiastic about the current executive. When I told her about the dream she replied with words to the effect of 'the chance of this lot resigning would be a fine thing!'. I laughed and commented on the stupidity of the dream, mentioning that it is not governments that resign, people do. A further two or three days later came the surprise announcement that the former Prime Minister of the United Kingdom, the person who we both associated with many of the issues that the country was facing, was resigning from his seat as a member of Parliament. Later that summer, my wife and I took a short boat trip along the river Trent in Newark, Nottinghamshire. We overheard a conversation between two staff members. One of them described a rare car that he had recently seen, a retro Lotus of a particular colour with very specific decals on it. The strange thing he said, was that he had dreamt of the exact same car a few days previously. His colleague seemed unimpressed with this story; however, little did they know that we were both very interested in pre-cognitive dreams and were fascinated by his story.

With topics such as pre-cognitive dreams, the easy option is to resort to the scepticism described earlier in respect of the collective unconscious. The negative reactions in both instances might be largely due to the social constructions of our materialist society. If, however, we take these topics seriously and seek opportunities to experience the effects for ourselves, then we might find ourselves accumulating evidence for a consciousness-situated ontology.

This morning, I am sat in another Sheffield *Kollective* café. It may well become my preferred writing location for this project. It is a little more peaceful here than in the fashionable establishment across the road that I wrote of earlier; the one which is very artsy and hip. This particular *Kollective* is the sister venue of the city centre one. It is located in a leafy suburb which is becoming extremely popular with ex-Londoners seeking affordable property in a location that they would be happy to call home. This leads me to a topic known to sociologists and others as *gentrification*. A recently published book *Gentrification Is Inevitable: and other lies* by Leslie Kern explores this phenomenon in more detail and it has an oblique relevance to the thesis being presented in this volume. Kern raises the question of whether or not the titular phenomenon is benevolent. Gentrification involves regenerating previously derelict parts of a city, which is initially taken as a positive development for obvious reasons. However, Kern argues that alongside the rebuilding there is often a social cleansing consequence, and also what she terms as exploitative side effects. For instance, many of the areas which are targets of gentrification, gain their initial cachet from the activities of artists, musicians, and ethnic minorities. In the southeast of England, past examples include Notting Hill (West Indians, musicians), Brick Lane (Asians) and Brighton (artists). Following gentrification, the original communities are often priced out of the area. To the untrained eye Kern suggests, it is initially difficult to determine the difference between the good of regeneration and the bad of exploitation. Many who are ultimately displaced by the high rents, well-heeled/good-taste residents, and high-price retail outlets often cheer the launch of the gentrification process. What appears visible to them initially, is money being injected into the area, activity, and shiny new stuff. Eventually, when the social cleansing phase has been completed, those original residents – now living elsewhere – come to understand the darker side of the phenomenon.

The socio-politics of gentrification is perhaps a useful metaphor to help understand the blurred lines between the true collective and the false one. The unreal collective offers that which initially gleams: beauty, newness, wealth; comfort. It is almost a natural reaction to be attracted to it. However, in the long term it is unlikely to be helpful to the well-being of an individual. Furthermore, the collective, described in the Vedanta and by Jung, is of the nature of the stuff from which reality is made. It is elemental to who we are, and indeed what we are. Despite our inability to fully elucidate its modus operandi, the philosophies described to this point suggest that it is of the utmost importance. Perhaps this is why the word spiritual is appropriate here; or moral if you prefer. The ontologically minded may interpret its importance as something to do with a greater reality perhaps. However, these are all simply words which attempt to capture the essence of that which the human intellect has yet to – or perhaps cannot – fathom. In this as yet unknown or even unknowable process of nature, perhaps communing is the goal – being as one; being together in love. To achieve this end, we need to somehow connect with the real collective, the unconscious one, the cloud of ineffability so elusive to conscious intention. As mentioned previously, the Vedantic sages described methods by which to move closer to the real, and these have been practised in certain communities for thousands of years. Some of these methods may be difficult to practise in the twenty-first century, given the quantity of distractions which are a feature of contemporary society. For example, the instructions outlined in the Bhagavad Gita for the practice of Raja Yoga (which is very meditation-focused) would be difficult to follow in a modern city, despite the current popularity of mindfulness in our era. However, the ancient Indians helpfully outlined *multiple* means to elevate consciousness, only one of which explicitly involves meditating. Another practice, known as *Karma Yoga,* is eminently suitable for the high-octane twenty-first century and can be incorporated into, for example, festival good times or while surrounded by the persistent noise of our epoch.

Occasions and Methods

> Art was not the goal but the occasion and the method for locating our specific rhythm and buried possibilities of our time. The discovery of a true communication is what it was about – or at least the quest for such a communication. (Steve Fitch, Waking Life, 2001).

I first watched Richard Linklater's millennial masterpiece *Waking Life* at the Curzon cinema on Shaftesbury Avenue, London in 2001. I have seen it many times since. The quote which opens this chapter had always intrigued and puzzled me. In the years when I was active in music, I had assumed that the art was the goal; that it was the beats, the bass and the melodies which were the object of our activity at those wonderful, creative gatherings. Indeed, this assumption is reflected in the way that the spaces which host these events are laid out, in the global west anyway. The band or DJ is often positioned front and centre, and the audience generally faces the artist. If this is considered a little more deeply, in the case of a DJ, it is unnecessary. There is not a great deal to see in a DJ performance, the sound is all that matters. However, there were hints of the *true* nature of these (Afro-diasporic inspired) events buried in my earliest experiences within the Caribbean community.

In these communities, the focus was upon the collective – there was no such thing as superstar DJs removed spatially, culturally, and economically from the audience. Back then, the music was provided by *sound systems* – themselves mini-collectives. Sound systems, however, were fully embedded into the community and the events at which they played, as opposed to being separate, like modern DJs. They didn't set up on a stage, rather they were usually to be found in a nook or corner. Thus, the sound crew were of the people and their primary role was to serve the group and initiate the collective magic. They were equals of the audience; it was a non-hierarchical relationship. An excellent academic examination of some of the social processes which operated within United Kingdom reggae sound systems of the nineteen seventies and early eighties (along with the scenes that followed: jungle and grime), can be found in Malcolm James' *Sonic Impact*. Perhaps the manner in which Afro-diasporic music events were organised offers deeper insight into the meaning of the Steve Fitch statement. The most important aspect of our coming together at the best parties and festivals is not the music and the dancing, as enjoyable as they might be. Perhaps these are sonic rituals which enable the true goal: collective communing. These situations enable exchange, oneness, and love. As the man said, the music events are simply the occasion, and the activities therein are the method. If this is in any way correct, then in theory at least, it should be possible to create the same communal magic in alternative situations on other occasions. There are not many spaces that are free from the dominance of the material mindset, and it would take quite an effort to reclaim any other normal mode of life from the capitalist-materialists. At the moment, and in large part thanks to the African diaspora, we have music, the rave, the shindig as a rare space, which is freer of the dominance of the false collective, where we can exercise the instincts of our truer nature. It is notable that when we return to our everyday lives on a Monday, we revert to viewing the party as something like a dream or illusion. This is back to front. Many of us implicitly know this and fantasise about living our lives in the mode of our (better) weekend or festival experiences. The opportunities to do so always seem limited.

Nevertheless, if this collective unconscious exists, then based upon the writings of those I have already mentioned, we are in constant communication with it at some level. The moments of Jungian synchronicity, the sharing of smiles with a stranger, the little acts of kindness, warmth, and genuine shared humour may all be instances of such. It is likely that many of us would long to develop this way of life, to be more open to the real, but the first step on this path would be to examine those aspects of existence which disrupt our ability to do this.

Inhibitors

This is an appropriate point at which to recognise the benefits of contemporary materialist science and technology. Very few among us exhibit the courage required to live without access to modern facilities. Fewer yet would choose to adopt the lifestyle of an ancient Indian sage; to suffer illness and death without the palliative procedures which are a part of our modern healthcare. It is safe to surmise that this is certainly not a life for the majority. That said, it is perhaps also important to recognise that life without such comforts was everyday reality for the many billions who lived in previous epochs, and indeed for many others in certain parts of the world today. Nevertheless, today we live better than kings and queens of old and any advocating for a return to a more simple and primitive mode of life is unlikely to be well received. The human mind has used its facility for logic to create these tools and services and most feel that they should be exploited for our personal benefit. An example, which particularly resonates, is that the understanding of quantum mechanics led to the invention of the transistor. The humble semiconductor is the technology on which modern amplifiers that power my party nights are built upon. A more prosaic example is that my good health is in part the result of the knowledge gained through the study of biology, chemistry and even engineering – modern sewers help keep us all healthy. Materialist science did all this.

In spite of the good that science and technology brings to modern society, it is nevertheless not unreasonable to draw attention to developments in these domains which may result in negative outcomes. In particular, I am considering material advancements which might – either as a side or a main effect – inhibit the human ability to interact with the collective that I am describing in this essay. These inhibitors might be grouped under the category of my term, the *false collective*. Of course, the collective is only a hypothesis, as is its material doppelganger. It is perfectly reasonable to choose to make a life based on the assumption that material existence is all there is. However, if such a route is chosen, meaning becomes harder to locate in one's life. Meaning is not material, it is ethical, moral, and/or spiritual. There is not enough space in this volume to embark upon an exploration of these topics. However, there are libraries full of philosophy – both ancient and modern – which relates to this area. I will simply say that perhaps the emptiness of the material mode of life is usefully illustrated by the occasional and well-publicised instances of wealthy individuals complaining of the lack of purpose in their lives. These people will have had the opportunity to explore every facet of the material lifestyle and will then have realised that it is ultimately empty. Episodes such as these reveal the long and tortuous road to the realisation that the unreal never is and the real never is not. It need not be this way, however. Philosophy allows one to reach the same conclusion without enduring numerous years of hollowness and angst.

It is time to begin exploring the false collective in more detail. In contrast to its transcendental sibling, this, I argue, is a human-curated and material domain which disrupts our ability to commune via the medium of love. I am writing this in the late summer of 2023, therefore the technologies in particular focus include the (perhaps fading) phenomenon of social media and the other (certainly *not* fading) contemporary marvel that is digital technology. The technological landscape, as is presently manifested, has been shaped by both the current dominant western political philosophy of *neo-liberal capitalism*, and the scientific gestalt of *materialism*. The latter might be likened to a medieval religious orthodoxy – we are all expected to believe in materialism and if we do not, then we are at best heretic, and at worst feeble-minded, or even lunatic. Most opt for the easier path of signing up to the proscribed philosophy. I, however, choose to demur. Of course, material is a real phenomenon of existence, but the difference between true believers and heretics is that the latter do not accept the position that material is the foundational layer of everything. The worldview of materialism demands of us that we accept that physical stuff is all there is.

The political philosophy of neo-liberal capitalism is not a belief system in the same vein as materialism. Rather, it is the framework upon which western societies hang their activities. It is the structure which forms the template of our lives. We do not need to believe in order to participate. Society is organised to coerce us into operating in this way. Even love is massaged to fit the framework. Therefore, love is recast as romantic or family love only. The romantic form is utilised in different ways, many of which ensure consumption and distraction. The nuclear family is also distractive (it ensures that love is restricted to a specific context). Another goal of family is offspring, which might perhaps be viewed through neo-liberal eyes as new material for the production-consumption treadmill. In this respect, education is regarded as a means to economic success. Its purpose – in the view of particular political philosophies – is to produce workers who will assist a society in its participation in the global game of GDP and finance. Entertainment is also now a neo-liberal instrument. It is the means to gather audiences who can be marketed to via advertisements. With the term *entertainment*, I am including the Internet, television, radio, and music events – including my beloved festivals. In fact, very many aspects of our lives are exploited in this way. If not for hard capitalist outcomes, then for the social conditioning necessary to maintain the framework. This latter is why the BBC exists.

Note that at this point it is important to make clear that this book is definitely not an exhortation to 'smash the system'. Any such system (or even the false collective if you like) will persist regardless of the efforts of disapprovers. If you 'smash' it, an equally powerful alternative will fill the void. See also the French and Russian revolutions. The same is true of societies that do not fit the western neo-liberal capitalist mode. Each has a political framework which is used to structure society. I do not assess the comparative merits and demerits of any political system, except to point out that their various philosophies, combined with scientific materialism, combined with the power of digital technologies, are likely to disrupt our ability to commune with the collective. Furthermore, as a citizen of a western economy, neo-liberalism is the particular configuration which I understand best. Therefore, my commentary is best consumed in the context of societies such as these. It is for this reason that neo-liberal capitalism features prominently in this thesis.

The Wasp

In the late summer of 2021, I attended *Tonnau*, a music festival which takes place on a beautiful country estate in north Wales. I had pitched my tent in what I thought was a peaceful and leafy part of the campsite, but my neighbours and I soon discovered that we were close to a very active wasp nest. It became a frequent topic of conversation amongst the campers. It was at this festival that I began sketching out some of the ideas that would become this book. As I observed the wasps, I developed a particular train of thought that was relevant to the themes I was exploring. Wasps are social insects. As I later discovered, their social behaviour predates ants and bees. However, as most of us are implicitly aware, there is a point in their life cycle where they become more selfish. This, I thought, might be an appropriate metaphor for the true collective versus the false one (and its associated focus on individualism). Afterwards, I contacted Seirian Sumner on Twitter (it was thus named back then). The Internet had suggested that she was an expert in all things wasp related. Professor Sumner kindly responded to my questions. Wasps, she wrote, are highly social during the early phase of the nest's development. Workers gather nectar, not for themselves (they cannot digest it) but for the grubs which are growing in cells. The workers receive a payback, however. When they deliver the nectar to the grubs, a sugary enzyme is released, which the worker insects love. This process ensures that the nest functions harmoniously and the new generation thrives. However, the grubs eventually reach a stage in their development where they no longer require nectar to be supplied to them, and with no sugary payback, the workers then become disconnected from their collective purpose. This is when we humans encounter them at their worst: buzzing around our beer and food; generally being a nuisance with a sting. Towards the end of a summer, one can find wasps descending to the level of the bluebottle – hovering around rotting food and ultimately, faeces. There may be a cautionary tale in the life cycle of the wasp – be part of the collective if you are able; otherwise shit awaits.

Capitalism's Leash

For the last century or so, western societies have adopted the narrative that it is the individual which is the locus of a well-lived life. This is broadly accepted until we are jolted out of the social construction by either a negative or a positive episode. A pertinent example might be a transformative experience at a music festival. Following such an event, one might explore philosophies and practices which promise pathways to the oneness of the collective. In previous times, those seeking a route to higher things were not confronted by a shower of distractions, such as twenty-four-hour news, sticky digital technology, and social media. Nevertheless, the processes outlined in the Vedantic texts, for example, are still valid in our shiny, contemporary world. The prerequisite to such practices in the digital era is perhaps to recognise and then nullify the distractions. In this, the media theorist Marshall McLuhan is a useful ally. His most famous work, *The Medium is the Massage*, was published long before the advent of internetworked computers. Much of the book is concerned with his contemporaneous electronic age of the nineteen sixties, but McLuhan also appeared able to foresee the trajectory of the innovations that surrounded him. It is a text about media in its purest sense; the vehicles through which messages are transmitted. For example, McLuhan presents the alphabet as medium, print technology as medium, and of course the electronic media of his time – notably television – as medium. The viewpoint represented in *The Medium is the Massage* can be summarised via the statement on page 68: 'environments are not passive wrappings but are, rather, active processes which are invisible'.

Those who seek to minimise the distractions of the false collective and tap into the unconscious community of the true will firstly need to make the invisible visible. The false collective is a cloud of communication. It is McLuhan's 'active environment' through which the orthodoxy of the society is promulgated, and the framework maintained. It is not simply neutral, nor is it 'just media' or 'tech' It is the material channels through which we all communicate, but not in the way that leads to *moksha* (the Sanskrit word for liberation). In fact, it is likely to lead to the slavery of consumerist individualism. The slavery of the wasp for sugar; for shit. It is as true of digital media as it was of television in McLuhan's time.

The smartphone is an attention-stealing device. It creates an environment for the senses which overrides the natural world that surrounds us and interrupts our inherent psychic processes. The world-wide web is built on hyperlinks – the clue of its disruptive nature is in the name: *hyper* linking. That is, distraction at a scale previously unknown. We, the users, will find ourselves hyper-jumping from one thing to another. The environment discourages settling, being at peace, and communing. This is before we even consider the philosophy and the political environment for which these new media have become the carrier waves. Hyper-flitting is the perfect vehicle for neo-liberal capitalism. A dearth of meditative communion also enables a radically materialist philosophy.

By way of an example, I am discovering that I am much more in a state of flow (see Csikszentmihalyi and LeFevre, 1989) while writing this essay using a pen and (paper) notepad. I have concluded that when I write on my computer, the subconscious awareness that addiction-satisfying experiences are just a click away – social hits, games, shopping, and news – will distract me and inhibit my ability to ponder things more deeply. Moreover, the device notifications ensure that I do not forget this. Therefore, during this particular writing project, my computer is switched off and my smartphone is out of reach. On this theme, some words that I wrote last summer are pertinent:

> As long as you keep your phone on your person, you are on capitalism's leash.
>
> How does it feel to be a house-trained poodle?

The goal then, is to learn to disconnect from the false collective as much as possible. Even amongst those who agree with the overall aim, it is likely that that there will be discomfort or dissonance regarding this. Deeply ingrained habits are not easy to break. To start with perhaps, learn how to detach from the materialistic framework in an environment in which you are fully engaged. A music festival is ideal, as is a concert, or relaxed social gathering. Any feeling of strangeness that is experienced might simply be the first perception of communication with the All. Transform that feeling into positive emotions; share thoughts, conversation with others. One of the problems of media and these artificial collectives is that they interrupt the more natural trains of thought. If, as Sheldrake suggests, the mind is not a self-contained computer, but rather a receiver that is tuned to a larger collective transceiver, then the false collective is a signal jammer. Instead of allowing the organic process of communication between the local and the remote to occur, it gets in the way, it adds a level of noise to the signal, overpowers the messages with external and unnatural content. What is this content exactly? It is the song of materialism: wealth, power, beauty, comfort, success. These signals bring to mind a concept from Vedantic philosophy – the *three gunas*. These are the illusions of the material world – 'darkness, passion and light' and while they are not wholly bad in themselves (light for instance, has many positive attributes), we are urged by the sages to rise beyond them. In effect, it is an exhortation to see beyond materialism and reside in a state of mind that is grounded in the All.

The signals of the false collective have always existed of course. In Roman society for instance, the lust for power and wealth was every bit as powerful as it is today. The difference is that I fear, and this is at the heart of this essay, digital technologies enable interference of a level and ubiquity previously unknown. The smartphone and its stickiness cause disruption to be ever present in our lives: at home, outside, first thing in the morning, last thing at night. The entire network of 4G and 5G masts, emerging like steel triffids across the country, can be considered the infrastructure of disruption. The smartphone/Internet combination would in itself be less disruptive if users were not drawn to these technologies compulsively. However, the applications built upon these platforms are designed to be addictive, so we tune in – morning, noon, and night.

Marshall McLuhan commented upon the multi-sensory nature of media and the way in which this becomes a virtual extension of our nervous system. The more senses that a medium communicates to, the greater the impact – or, in the terms of this thesis – disruption. In the early twentieth century, the landscape already included portable media; that is, newspapers. However, these appealed to a single sense only – vision, and much of the content was textual. Furthermore, newspapers had no method for generating the stickiness that modern technologies achieve. One would read the paper, usually in the morning, and the interaction would end there. Compare and contrast to contemporary media use.

TV Gotcha Now

Educated one

You of refinement
And know-how
Cultured
Erudite
Or should I say
Savoir-faire.

I ran with you
In the nineties
From Woodstock Road
To The Strand
And in the lovely Lanes.

Oh, how you despised
Television.

TV.
The – what was it –
Opiate of the masses?
You – we –
Were so much better
We didn't have
TVs.

If we did
It was a tiny
Portable thing
Maybe even
Black and white
And stored in a cupboard
In case of events
Of significant magnitude

Books
You said.
Broadsheets.
Cafés and culture
Theatre, cinema
And nightclubs

TV?
You laughed
Plebsville
A life wasted.

But brother,
My sister
Ain't it the truth that
TV Gotcha Now.

It changed
It
Outsmarted
You
It did a little side shimmy
and changed its form
Tablet
Mobile
Social.

Ah.

TV's gotcha hooked like drugs
Now.
Everywhere you go
You got TV
The channels have
Morphed
Shape-shifted;
FacebookTwitterYouTubeInstagram
New Channels
New TV
And you can't escape

In your cosy little cafés
You've got TV
In your bookshops.
In your theatres and cinemas
You must be told
To turn off your TV

Yes my friend
TV gotcha now
TV gotcha bad.

In the nineteen nineties my social circle was largely composed of educated urbanites. I recall that at that time, there was a tendency to regard those who watched significant amounts of television with scorn. Those friends of mine read literary novels and quality newspapers, they enjoyed highbrow theatre productions, and attended music performances. One particular Oxford-based associate kept a portable black and white TV unit in a cupboard which she would only bring out if events of a sufficient magnitude warranted it. The inspiration for my poem *TV Gotcha Now* was observing the growth of a new form of 'television' which entirely sidestepped the snobbery of this intelligent and self-congratulatory social group. It was fascinating to watch the new media slowly exert a grip as firm as the one with which the old goggle box had dominated the lives of what they considered to be the less enlightened social classes. This cautionary tale is the story of us all. The new media, the Internet, smartphone, digital technology is now all-pervasive. There were particular features of the new technologies which enabled this victory, and I will outline some of them in a subsequent section. A key inflection point can be detected in the period following the millennium when various new features of web design were adopted. These were dubbed *web 2.0*. In 2010, the technologist Jaron Lanier published a polemic entitled *You Are Not a Gadget*. It was in part an attempt to warn society about the unforeseen consequences of what he, and his colleagues had just unleashed. The original World Wide Web (that is, the web methodology up to the year two thousand and retrospectively referred to as *web 1.0*) was obviously a great deal simpler than that which surrounds us today. It was predominantly text-based and less reactive. Web 1.0 was egalitarian – organisations had yet to establish a dominant presence in the way they have today. There was little difference between the structure of a commercial website and a private one. Users of the early Internet contributed to the corpus through the creation of their own web pages and web sites. These were usually hand-coded in raw HTML, and hyperlinks were manually added, pointing visitors to other sites and pages that each creator was particularly fond of.

Web 1.0 was very human, and I am nostalgic for that Internet. It had few of the ease-of-use or algorithmic features that abound today. Tracking cookies, for example, were introduced in web 2.0. I summarise the difference between web 1.0 and web 2.0 as follows. The first version was a tool which helped to enhance true collective communing. It brought individuals together for the purpose of exchanging ideas and love. There was little manipulation of that interaction – it occurred organically. Web 2.0 was designed to amplify the processes of the false collective. It sought to bring people together in a more contrived fashion, manipulated by the algorithm and was chiefly concerned with neo-liberal outcomes. For sure, with effort, this later version of the web can be used to support true communion. However, without such awareness, and simply using the Internet in the way in which it presents itself to us, will result in the opposite.

If today an individual walked past a newspaper stall and read the headlines, it is unlikely that there would be a single header concerned with the reader's personal well-being, growth, or any higher outcomes. Headlines are a useful exemplifier of the processes which I am describing – they generally seek to arouse, manipulate, and set the mind to the domain of the false collective: things you want, things you don't like, tribalism. Regarding the latter, the popular tribalism of team sports is worth dwelling upon for a little while longer. In the United Kingdom football (or soccer for those west of the Atlantic Ocean) is especially noteworthy in this regard. Indeed, in the nineteen eighties, this tribalism regularly spilled over into violence. It wasn't always so. Prior to the capture of this pastime by neo-liberal agents, football was an activity with communing and community at its heart. There is an obscure made-for-television film entitled *The World Cup: A Captain's Tale* starring Dennis Waterman of *Minder* and *The Sweeney* fame. It is a humble production but can be recommended for various aspects. The work is primarily an entertainment, but it also emphasises both the history and sociology of the sport. It serves as a reminder that the sport was once a vehicle for the collective. That is, win or lose, or the performance of one's favoured team was only incidental to the collective communing which the activity was the occasion for. I have often mused on the similarity between the best aspects of grass roots sporting communities and the Caribbean sub-culture that I grew up as a part of. In both situations, the purveyors of the activity (footballers or DJs) were not elevated to distant celebrity; it was always the *community* which occupied centre stage. For various reasons – primarily (but not exclusively) neo-liberal capitalism – football has in large part associated itself with the false collective. If due care and attention is not applied, a supporter may be dragged into the less benevolent orbit of betting websites, mass-produced alcohol products, and highly questionable foreign regimes.

Nevertheless, even in environments where the processes of the false collective dominate, I would argue that it is still possible to commune organically, if enough of those who are alive to the possibilities come together. Indeed, my writing of this book in the midst of a society which is held in the sway of the unreal, is an example of this point. That is, I am aware of an audience who may respond positively to these ideas – they motivate me, and I in turn will hopefully inspire them. These easily overlooked interactions are important because other occasions for collective coming together, for example, music festivals, are becoming increasingly coerced by capitalist organisations. Earlier this summer at my annual pilgrimage to WOMAD in Wiltshire, United Kingdom, I (and others) was a little dismayed to discover a large and unashamedly corporate *Lush Cosmetics* store at one end of the camping field. In fairness, such capitalist incursions have been a feature of festivals for as long as I have been attending them. There is always a strand of hard commerce that runs a little beneath the ostensible 'peace and love' ambience. WOMAD, along with other similar happenings, exists in a world of realpolitik and finance. It requires considerable sums of money to organise an event of such scale. Capitalist enterprises are keen to hijack the communal spirit of love that are characteristic of such events and pay handsomely to be able to disrupt and redirect those feelings into commercial wins. The artists and the audience create the special aura (which is actually a cloud of unconscious communing) and the capitalists inject the messages of the false collective in order to achieve their specific ends (power, money, etc.). The funds which big businesses inject into the festival, cover the considerable costs – including artist fees. It is the job of those of us who are seeking to reduce the influence of the false collective in our lives to dance around the unreal, the V.I.P. areas, vanity, and mirrors (you really don't need a mirror at a festival – it's about the inner not the outer). The key is to avoid bear traps such as these and continue to share, communicate, and spread love. In my view there are certain items which have no place at a festival if it is to be used as an environment to aim higher. These include smartphones, newspapers, and perhaps even coffee (but more of that later).

Despite the best efforts of the neo-liberal capitalist brigade, the genuine magic of the festival persists. Furthermore, it is often only truly established late at night. In the wee hours, the scheduled events have ended and the stalls selling goods have shut for the night. Even Lush Cosmetics is closed, dark and empty save for the lonely security guard, sat in the gloom scrolling through his smartphone to alleviate the boredom. The presence of the guard indicates the assumption of the capitalists that we, the night-time revellers, would seek to storm their citadel of material and steal its treasures should the chance arise. However, late at night there are in fact treasures of a completely different nature that we avail ourselves of. Between one and perhaps eight a.m., the false collective is sleeping and in the DJ tents, the little obscure cafés, and the hidden after-party locations there is magic. Here, there be dancing, sharing, and communication on a scale rarely seen in everyday life. This indeed, is one of Rachel Horne's spaces that break the rules of modern life. Spliffs are being passed from the lips of one stranger to another as are bottles of wine and phials of vodka. Expressions of love between strangers; conversation – deep and honest and true. Sparks of synchronicity fire off in every direction, and on waking the following day one can hardly believe that it actually happened. Yes, people here take drugs, they are intoxicated on alcohol. However, even with that being so (and it is not always the case) the experiences are of a very different timbre to the world of the everyday, the false collective. Perhaps if we were able to mute the incessant noise of the false in our quotidian existence, we might experience such magic on a more regular basis – not only at festivals.

In all of this speculation regarding the collective unconscious and its possible effects, I hope that I have made clear that the material layer exists – I am no solipsist! In the same way that the experience of an optical illusion exists – the optical effect itself might be illusory, but our experience of it is not – so too material existence. The material layer determines much of the felt qualities of our lives. A plausible argument might be made that materialism and capitalism in fact *enable* certain qualities of our world which enhance communication with the collective. For example, the capital which brings the music festivals to life, or the advanced understanding of biology and chemistry, combined with engineering and sewerage technology which help to keep me healthy enough to go out and dance all night. Nevertheless, and here is a dichotomy, the noise of the false collective has become excessively shrill. A little, or even middling amounts of interference are to be expected, indeed, it is part of the challenge of life. Modern digital information technologies, however, have created a ubiquitous dominance of the unreal, such that it suffocates opportunities to commune in any other way. The silence and peace which can enable the transmission and reception functions of Sheldrake's transceivers, are more difficult to find today.

Some might propose that a solution to this state of affairs is to seek to dismantle the false collective. We can be certain that such an idea will be vehemently resisted by those who profit from its distracting methods. This resistance will take the form of propaganda, ideology, and messaging – and possibly worse. I cannot foresee a situation where a philosophy of a naturalistic collective unconscious will be allowed to replace the profitable materialist structures that have been carefully nurtured over the last couple of centuries. Here then is the challenge. The African slaves and their descendants were able to subvert some of the powerful structures which surrounded them via the wonderful consciousness technologies unleashed through their music (see the chapter *Black Music As Psychic Technology*). However, that was then. The question is how do we, in the twenty twenties achieve a similar goal, on a wider scale, with psychological tools of great potency ranged against such efforts.

Paradoxes

The blurring of the lines between good and bad, the benevolent and the malevolent is an important topic which is touched upon at various points in this essay. The truth is that things are rarely, if ever, wholly good, or wholly bad. This paradox should be taken into account during decision-making. It is important because in the good there is some bad, and in the bad there is some good. Simple examples will illustrate this point. Nuclear power can be considered good, primarily because it is a power source that is not based on fossil fuels and therefore does not contribute greenhouse gases to the atmosphere. Therefore, for this reason it can be said to be environmentally friendly. Nevertheless, it also creates a different, pervasive form of pollution in terms of radioactive nuclear waste which remains harmful for thousands of years. This is to say nothing of the potential for catastrophic accident, or the apocalyptic military by-products of the refinement process. An even more obvious example of this type of paradox is fire, the discovery of which was a game-changer for humankind. It enabled a more varied diet and provided power, warmth, and light. In later generations we used it to generate steam and therefore drive machines for transportation and manufacturing. Even now, the little blue flame in our gas boilers and cooking stoves are testament to the enduring usefulness of fire. On the other hand, forest fires, house fires, and firestorms in war zones are wholly problematic. Such paradoxes are difficult to resolve. Leaping feet first into absolute judgements can be dogmatic and extreme and it is rarely a valid position to adopt.

Kastrup

If the theories of Bernardo Kastrup are in any way accurate then all is consciousness. The reason for his statement 'materialism is baloney' is because it is a philosophy which is based on representation rather than true reality. Kastrup breaks this down well and I shall make an attempt to summarise his position. Reality is what we experience. Good science is empirical which means that it is based on experience. Importantly, science must also be as sophisticated as possible in interpreting these experiences, otherwise the naive errors outlined at the start of this book will obscure truth. Experiences are located in consciousness: the smell of a rose, the feel of suede, the sound (or bodily perception) of a reggae bassline. The weight of a metal bar. Science uses numbers to represent these sensations, for example, the frequency and timings of the bass notes or the mass in kilograms of the metal bar. To avoid becoming embroiled in a complex philosophical discussion, it is enough to say that materialist science, according to Kastrup, has evolved from using the numbers as a simple shorthand for the conscious experience, to assuming that the shorthand *is* the material reality itself. This is because over the years materialism has developed a worldview which no longer accepts the primacy of consciousness. Material is all that it admits, and worse yet, because material is only knowable (according to this viewpoint) via measurement, only the *measurable* aspects of material exist. Therefore, material which exhibits measurable properties including length, weight, height, mass, velocity, and spin are real. When challenged to explain consciousness, materialists become a little lost, arguing that it is only an *epiphenomenon* of material. Thus, in respect of human mental life, the principal material of interest to researchers of this ilk is the brain, and its physical structure formed of neurons and electrons, for example. All measurable.

Love, in this material view, is not primary or real, it is an epiphenomenon. It is unmeasurable, therefore viewed with intense suspicion. The reason that Bernardo Kastrup is a hero to many, is because it appears that he is brave enough to stand up to the many who support the materialist edifice and accuse the emperors therein of parading unclothed. Due to my Afro-diasporic upbringing, my reading of Indian philosophy from an early age, as well as an interest in psychology (Jung, Freud etc.), I am inclined to agree with him. It is fair to say that I do not fully understand the materialist mindset. I have not lived it. I have not filtered existence through that particular gestalt. Kastrup argues that ostensible materialists are in fact not materialists in their everyday lives. How could they then profess love to a partner? 'The epiphenomenon in my brain is causing pleasurable sensations when I think of you my dear'. Most will live as deeply in their conscious experiences as any other person. The problem is that due to the combination of the materialist paradigm and the socio-economic and political framework that we exist within, we construct an individualistic world which functions as though consciousness is the by-product of material. Therefore, there is no communing, there is no collective. We are self-contained material processing units. Stimulus and response. Electrical signals in our brains. Computers. This viewpoint also encourages those who feel that one day we may be able to commune with machines and artificial social stimuli as successfully, and as rewardingly as in our communion with other living things. A central misunderstanding of the digital era.

(In Praise of) Human Curation

Driven by the need for
Ease and profit
We find ourselves
Here where
Human curation is a rare thing.

We are awash with
Automation-curation
Devoid of soul.
And arid.

When we eventually
Become aware that we are
Collective;
Communing constantly, and
That we are connected in an
Ineffable way,
Then we understand that
Automated/curated
Is empty and pointless.
Sans art or meaning.

Automation is
The aping of the real –
Monkey see, monkey do –
All form.
Faux function.

Human curation
On the other hand
Activates connection
Between us.
And the beauty experienced
By curator and recipient
Is an echo of the sublime
Reality which determines
Our alpha

And omega.

The notion of the collective implies that there is a qualitative difference between the communication which occurs amongst living things, and human interaction with pseudo or digital entities. For instance, if Kastrup is correct and we are all dissociated segments within a universal mentation, then human inter-communication occurs amongst segmented parts of that greater self. This implies that digital interaction with artificial entities is of a wholly other nature. Instead of having a conversation with a real person, one who is literally cut from the same psychic cloth, you instead enter into a transaction with a cartoon animation which is designed to imitate human reactions. You cannot share love with a machine, and it cannot do the same for you. There is nothing higher or deeper. Vedantic texts argue that the most profound communion with others (by which they imply the sharing of love) instigates valuable psychic processes of a nature not fully understood. These are said to ennoble us and lead to beneficial spiritual outcomes. There are additional advantages in the quotidian existence too; mental health and positive emotions, for example. Experiences such as these would probably be placed in the epiphenomenon category by hard materialists, but I would challenge the most ardent amongst them to deny the importance of such feelings.

I cannot claim any special understanding of the collective. I can hypothesise, drawing on the likes of Jung, Sheldrake, and Kastrup. I can also convey the aphoristic conclusions of Vedantic texts, and this is the extent of my contribution. Nevertheless, the cumulative weight of hint and insight from theorists, sages, and experiencers (of near death or psychedelics) may be sufficient for us to take a chance and live as though the collective matters. Fortunately, when we do this, we are rewarded with returns of positive emotions and synchronicity. At this point we might perhaps begin to gain a greater understanding of why the solitary wasp descends to shit, and why the communing human tends to enlightenment and joy. The truth may be found through the experience. It is a different kind of empiricism. An empiricism of the within; of consciousness – not the observed if-then causality of the material domain.

When I embarked upon writing this text, I was still infused with visions of that collective. I had recently returned from a festival where I had experienced that communal spirit first-hand, and I was therefore in touch with the phenomena associated with it. Since then, sadly, I have re-immersed myself in the world and its daily grind. As much as I have attempted to retain the high of that collective experience, it fades. Therefore, the descriptions of the collective being offered at this point in my writing are from memory and not from any inner sight. The key Vedantic text, the Bhagavad Gita refers to this state of affairs. It distinguishes between those who speak about the universal All from direct vision, versus recollection, versus those who have heard about it from others. In addition to this, in the same text we find a quite profound verse which offers the metaphor of the soul being like a lake. The suggestion being that the lake bed (Brahman) can only be seen when the lake is still. This stillness is achieved when we live and think in a soulful way. If we were to realise how simple it is to access the magic of the All, we might not choose to thread our most profound experiences through the interpretive mangle of materialism. Our primary concern would be others, and not just others as stand-alone entities; rather the *connection* between ourselves and those others. Moreover, once those connections are realised, we would then ascertain their purpose: conduits through which we push love from us to them.

A short paragraph on wrongness is required here; badness, evil – call it what you will. Frankly, it is not an area that I understand well. The Vedantic texts put negative traits down to ignorance; in their terms, the agitation of the lake and losing sight of the real (the bed of the lake). Once vision is thus obscured, it is easy to become prey to destructive emotions: lust, greed, and ignorance. From this scenario emerges wrongness. In terms of our encounters with those operating in this mode, it is quite likely that we might receive only hostility from them, especially where we are attempting to activate a connection. This does happen and we need to be streetwise. It should not, however, discourage us from pushing love along those conduits, no matter who the recipient of that love is. It is good to remind ourselves of Kastrup's view that we are all sectioned off parts of a whole. That wrong'un also resides in the greater you; the universal transpersonal mentation. I and I, Ubuntu, the collective unconscious. Additionally, I do find that when connection is activated, even with a wrong'un, moments of surprising warmth can sometimes ensue.

****

It is a Monday morning. I generally avoid writing over the weekend, and this allows me the time to pause and think about areas that I wish to explore in the coming week. Today I am in a famous Sheffield café named *Bragazzi's* on Abbeydale Road. It is lacking the serenity of my usual haunt,

Kollective. However, today the latter is closed, and sadly the atmosphere in here is very rooted in the material. There are large groups of men being quite macho, which disturbs my serenity a little. It is not normally like this in here. To borrow a lyric from George Harrison, we are living in the material world and the challenge for us all is to attempt to rise above it.

The theme of the weekend was the idea that friends can be enemies, and enemies can be friends. By this I am referring to situations where you are surrounded by people or things that you ostensibly do not like – for example, places that are not the preferred environment for whatever it is that you are into. However, unknown to the individual in question, that particular situation might be one where the collective consciousness is thriving. Conversely, one might find oneself in another environment that feels comfortable, reading media that an individual thinks reflects their mindset. However, this setting may be far from being conducive to true collective communing. Here our hypothetical person might be surrounded by the false collective. Be aware therefore, of false friends. The point is that discrimination is important, as is awareness and vigilance. It is not easy to exercise these attributes constantly, but nothing worthwhile is easy, of course.

As an example of the above, consider the following. Thoughtful and sensitive individuals generally accept the concept of *diversity* as positive. Byung-Chul Han discusses a number of contemporary ideas, including *authenticity* and *diversity* in the light of his criticisms of neo-liberal capitalist societies. He argues that 'diversity ... constitutes an otherness that has been made consumable'. To put it differently, the discourse of diversity is a neo-liberal capitalist discourse, useful to the political and economic ends of this framework. According to Han, true variety is found in the concept he describes as *otherness* which is less cuddly and acceptable – it is jarring, frightening even. Otherness, according to Han, is not meant to be universally palatable; rather, it challenges. It is also essential to a full life. This philosopher argues that capitalism attempts to portray otherness in cartoon fashion, names it *diversity*, and somehow expects the result to be peace and harmony. If anything, this neo-liberal diversity sows discord. It is an attempt to coalesce society around a concept which is ultimately a lie. This then is the false collective in parasite mode, entering our communities via a seemingly innocuous discursive payload.

The Golden Thread

This is an idea I had once on a long flight about the connection between us all. The names I have mentioned a few times previously – that is, Rupert Sheldrake, C. G. Jung, Bernardo Kastrup, and the ancient anonymous Vedantic sages – describe this concept in their different ways. The notion that there are ties which attach us to each other is in itself significant. Thus, we are not isolated individuals, and the individualist-materialist mode that we are coerced to exist within can be viewed to be false. The thread of course is a metaphor. Kastrup as we know, describes this effect as dissociative boundaries within a whole. For Jung and Sheldrake this effect comes about through a shared or collective unconsciousness or memory. However, in addition to being a join, the thread is also a conduit. More than a simple metaphor to represent attachment, it is also an exhortation to action. It allows us to – indeed insists that we – push love through it from one to another, to another. Here is the purpose of the thread, the purpose of life. We should perhaps speak less of *spreading* love and more of *pushing* love. Human – specialist – pusher. Our purpose. The science fiction writer Robert Sheckley realised this (and here, as I write, is a moment of synchronicity) in his short story *Specialist*.

When I watch adverts which attempt to highlight our separateness, I am dismayed. Meditating on our connectedness while the marketing material appears on the television screen, I realise that (from the perspective of the collective) it is as mendacious a message as it is possible to send. They are falsehoods from which various individuals and groups seek to gain. That which they seek to gain is nothing in the true (non-material) reality. Thus, they are creating illusions for the purpose of reaping illusions. My advice would be this – don't be hoodwinked. Seek truth in the midst of lies.

I am very aware that I am rehearsing grand sentiments in this section, yet offering no real guidance as to how to incorporate them into a twenty-first century life. I intend to make a stab at the practical implications of the philosophy being described (if you can call it such) in later sections. Nevertheless, even without action, simply considering these concepts is a useful exercise because it helps one to differentiate between the real and the unreal, truth and falsity. Having said this, action remains key. We can describe and ponder the taste of the fruit, nevertheless the actual tasting of the food is the lived experience.

Comfort is a cage, happiness is the lure – (Professor Tara Brabazon).

This recently minted aphorism struck me as containing a certain truth when I encountered it on the Internet in the summer of 2022. I found myself creating derivatives to reflect more accurately what I was thinking about at the time. For example:

Neo-liberal capitalism is a cage, comfort is the lure

However, in the context of this volume, perhaps the following is most apt (although certainly not the most poetic):

Individualistic materialism is a cage, the false collective is the lure

The false collective pulls us in. It creates a material community and conversation around things that are not true. It celebrates the political philosophy (neo-liberal capitalism) and the ontology of our times (materialism). The discourses permitted within the false collective create the sense that there is nothing but this. Love as epiphenomenon. It has lured us into that cage and behind us, the door is slammed shut. For as long as we choose to attach ourselves to the untruths, we remain in the cage. Often, we are fully aware of the limiting philosophical nature of the life that we lead, but we choose to remain caged. The method of opening the door (which is in fact always unlocked) is to simply direct oneself towards the All, the *transmentation*. It is a combination of firstly recognising that it exists – or even taking a chance on the possibility that it might – and then directing one's activity towards that, rather than the falsehood. This will necessitate a rewiring of one's social relations and sometimes one's environment. Fortunately, the reward is always worthwhile. Changes will occur in the quality of life. The Bhagavad Gita – and Juan Mascaró's introduction to the 1962 edition – offer poetic meditations on this subject.

In Byung-Chul Han's words 'we live today in the neo-liberal system which breaks down temporally stable structures, fragments living-time and permits the *disintegration of what binds us together* in the interests of increasing productivity' (Han, p. 33 – the italics are mine). What 'binds us together' may in fact be the collective.

The *false* collective may not be a collective at all, rather simply the nihilistic phenomenon of mass individualism.

Of Double Slits and Knowing

About ten years ago, I started to write a novel. It was to have been titled *The Schrödinger Strain*. Sadly, it will never see the light of day, but the book was intended as a vehicle for an idea that struck me after my reading of an introductory text on quantum mechanics – one that I actually understood. One of the original mysteries in this field is the outcome of what is known as the *double slit experiment*. I shall do my best to summarise. An electron gun is placed opposite a screen and fires electrons at it. The screen is made of material which will indicate the point at which each electron lands. Between the electron gun and the screen there is a barrier with two slits, A and B. These will allow the electrons to pass through and make the marks on the screen. The electron gun fires the particles slowly so that they can be seen appearing one by one on the screen.

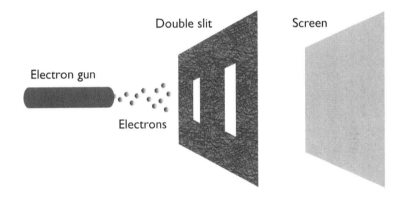

Figure 2. Double-slit experiment

Initially, the observer notes the electrons creating individual and isolated marks on the screen. When a substantial number of electrons have been fired, what is called an *interference pattern* develops. This is characterised by a distinctive banding arrangement of the marks, but also – and importantly – a large number of points appear *between* slit A and slit B (see figure 3). Why? One would expect the largest number of points to be detected opposite each of the slits.

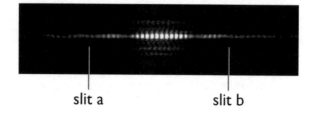

slit a   slit b

Figure 3. Double slit interference pattern

If the experiment is repeated with one of the slits closed, say slit B, we note that the majority of marks fall as expected, opposite slit A (see figure 4.)

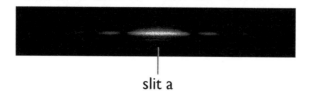

slit a

Figure 4. Single slit pattern

Quantum Theory: A Very Short Introduction by John Polkinghome describes the mystery of the double slit experiment. Had the electron passed through slit A it would have marked the screen opposite slit A. The same is true in the case of slit B. Why then the mass of points *between* slit A and slit B? The only conclusion is that each (non-divisible) electron passed through both slits. As Polkinghome admits, this is a nonsense conclusion in respect of normal logic and classical physics but is typical of quantum weirdness. Quantum scientists do not know what this means. It is simply accepted.

The other puzzling aspect of this experiment is as follows. If detectors are placed next to each slit to attempt to determine exactly where an electron is at any given point in time, sometimes an electron would be detected near slit A and sometimes near slit B. Here comes the weirdness: this added measurement also has the effect of destroying the interference pattern. With detectors in place, most of the marks will be either opposite slit A or slit B as in the single slit test.

Thus unobserved, electrons act in a weird and indeterminate manner, but upon observation they fall into line and behave as we might expect. This effect has flummoxed some of the best minds of the past century. There have been various hypotheses put forward to explain this phenomenon. However, none have wholly satisfied the scientific community and furthermore, if correct, some would have metaphysical ramifications of quite an unprecedented magnitude.

My novel-that-never-was, *The Schrödinger Strain*, attempted to build an entertaining fictional tale which coalesces the mystery of the double slit experiment with the ever-increasing observation, and *knowing* that is at the core of the hyper-information society. The double slit mystery suggests that if we do not observe the position of the electron, the particle manifests all possibilities and probabilities. It is only when we *know*, do the probabilities collapse into a single specific actuality. Thus, when we do not know, the world is rich with potentiality. One of the explanatory hypotheses of the *measurement problem* as this is sometimes known, is the *many worlds* hypothesis. This suggests that the multiple probabilities are in fact real. Once an observation is made, and an actual position of the electron is ascertained, the other possibilities spin off and occur in other parallel and disconnected universes. Bernardo Kastrup has no time for this. He suggests the idea is 'baloney' and isn't exactly parsimonious as good theory should be. Many others struggle with the ontological ramifications of the idea. Kastrup regards the measurement problem of quantum mechanics as a further hint that reality is primarily consciousness. One theoretical explanation for the double slit observation effect is that at the end of every chain of observation is consciousness. We only know the position of the particle because we become aware of the detector reading. This leads some to suggest that the collapse of potentiality is indicative of reality being curated by consciousness. In other words, material phenomenology at the particle scale is unformed until consciousness defines the outcome.

The idea of the primacy of consciousness is also suggested by Gary Lachman for different reasons. In his *Dreaming Ahead of Time*, he argues that pre-cognitive dreams – an everyday phenomenon apparently – are simply the dream consciousness accessing the reality-forming processes that underlie all consciousness. It is a hint that reality is not what it seems. Illusions; the primacy of mentation. Ideas which perhaps Kastrup may be sympathetic towards.

To return to *The Schrödinger Strain*. The central idea was that if observation or knowing affects the reality of atomic particle behaviour, what impact does our hyper-knowledge society have? The novel was named after the famous thought experiment (conceived by quantum physicist Erwin Schrödinger) involving a hypothetical cat in a hypothetical box alongside hypothetical radioactive material. The cat is both alive and dead (depending on the unknown state of the radioactive material), until the point at which we open the box and observe it. When we look in the box, the potentialities collapse, and the cat takes on a single state of either alive or dead. We might update this for the age of digital social media as follows.

In a previous epoch, a young person may have sent a *billet-doux* to an admired other. The young person sending the love letter would be in a state of ignorance regarding whether their intended had responded positively or negatively to the declaration of love. It could take weeks for the stagecoach (let us assume the early nineteenth century) to deliver the missive, and even more time for the other to craft their reply and for this to be returned to the original sender. In all this time there is a wealth of potentiality. The cognitive equivalent of electrons is pregnant with potentiality. The nineteenth-century world of our would-be lover is full of either/or states. Today, in the age of gigabytes-per-second communication, such potentiality disappears. Communication between *des amants* is today performed on messaging apps. One immediately knows if the message has been delivered and when the other party has read it. There are far fewer Schrödinger boxes in our world. Cats are either alive or dead. Potentiality is a rare phenomenon. And what of particles? All this observation, all this *knowing* – are electrons in the indeterminate state as abundant as they used to be? The *Schrödinger Strain* was a tale about how the lack of potentiality gave rise to a previously unknown ailment which developed in those who were exposed to large amounts of information. In the novel, hyper-observation was discovered to have altered something fundamental in the behaviour of atomic particles within human beings.

It was fiction of course, and I hoped I could create a ripping science-fiction yarn, with an added soupçon of philosophical plausibility. However, I think I have realised that I am not a novelist. Polemics such as this one are more my forte. The purpose of the detour into unfinished novels and quantum mechanics is to play with the idea that the false collective may, in addition to disrupting the true collective being defined in this essay, also have other effects, which we are yet to comprehend. Information overload may have profound ramifications.

Within and Without

Byung-Chul Han invokes the philosopher Heidegger to compare the *within* to the *without*. Here is one of the paradoxes that are often encountered in this topic area. In using the term *within*, Han and Heidegger are referring to the inner self which is the part of ourselves that is connected to the greater consciousness. By contrast, the *without* is related to the external material existence:

> Heidegger's dasein ... is guided not from without but from within. It resembles a gyrocompass, with an inner centre and a strong orientation towards its own potentiality-for-being. In this it is the opposite of distracted radar-humans who lose themselves outwards (Han, p. 32).

In the twenty-first century, the radar which distracts contemporary society has been constructed from digital technology using a neo-liberal capitalist blueprint. Han also describes one of the objects of this distraction, 'other people'. He implies that other people are not distracting per se, it is only when we and they are part of a society which is structured along the lines of the false collective, do social groupings become especially problematic. The false narrative turns others into a source of competition and angst instead of a target of love.

> Inward orientation renders superfluous the constant comparison with other people to which humans guided from without are compelled ... Today many people are plagued with diffuse fears: fear of failure, fear of falling behind, fear of making a mistake or the wrong decision ... This anxiety is reinforced by a constant comparison with others (Han, p.32).

An environment in which comparison comes easily is a cornerstone of neo-liberal capitalism, of hyper-marketing, and of the advertisement paradigm. This was a powerful methodology in the electric/electronic age with television, billboards, and colour print media. The digital revolution has created an even more invasive, ever-present theatre of self-judgement, which we are compelled to inhabit. This environment is the false collective and it insists that we live in the *without* rather than the *within*.

The *within* is that meditative zone where the inner connects to the greater outer; that is, the All. The within is what The Bhagavad Gita designates *Atman* and has been described as 'the divine spark within us all'. The paradox is that *Atman* is also *Brahman*. This latter is everything; the universal. Brahman, in Vedantic literature, is considered to be the Godhead at the apex of the cosmos and this idea resonates with the western aphorism 'the kingdom of heaven is within you'. The phrase is found in the Christian New Testament (Luke 17:21) It is also the title of a book by Leo Tolstoy and additionally, features as a repeated lyric in the 1970 Funkadelic recording, *Free Your... Mind and Your Ass Will Follow*. Note that this is a subtle notion, and it needs to be considered fully in order to avoid confusing its meaning. That the Atman is part of Brahman does not mean that we are gods. The Atman within can be likened to a Kastrupian dissociated alter, gazing at its own lake bed (as in the metaphor described earlier), which is Brahman. Brahman is ever-present, but we can only be fully aware of it when the surface of the lake is still. When the lake is agitated, we cannot know the greater consciousness. This is similar to our being distracted by the false collective. The stillness of the within, the peace that the practice of pushing love through the conduits of the golden thread engenders, aids the calm which helps the lake bed to become visible. Only then can we honestly speak of the connection between our personal Atman and Brahman.

In the language of Kastrup then, Atman is comparable to a dissociated alter and Brahman the universal transmentation of which the alters are a part. In the alternative language of Jung and Sheldrake, Brahman is that collective unconscious, which we neither fully perceive nor understand. Atman is to do with our individually situated consciousness which can, given the right conditions, connect to the collective. The reoccurrence of similar ideas in various cultures perhaps gives clues about their universality and possible veracity. From Rastafarians in Jamaica through to Ubuntu in Africa, the Amerindians, ancient Greeks, plus the more recent thinkers mentioned in this text. In addition to this, it is especially noteworthy that the burgeoning literature in the area of near-death experiences (NDEs) frequently contain reports of situations where the subject feels a sense of oneness with all living things. Even psychonauts – those who consume powerful psychoactive substances in order to explore other modes of consciousness – return from their trips with accounts of cosmic oneness. Perhaps of interest then is that in addition to the philosophical, scientific, and technical accomplishments of Bernardo Kastrup, it is also well known that he is a psychonaut, and this informs aspects of his thinking. In his *Ways to Go Beyond* volume, Rupert Sheldrake described how he dropped acid as an undergraduate student at

Cambridge. This summer at the WOMAD music festival, I was waiting in line for the toilets near *Molly's Bar*. A young girl joined the queue behind me and, as is the way at festivals, we struck up a conversation. It was a fairly unremarkable chat until she announced that she was 'tripping'. As this book was already beginning to take shape in my head, I was interested – particularly when she explained that she was trying to work out where she ended, and where the rest of the world began. Aha, I thought, oneness is everywhere. Perhaps psychedelics fracture what my favourite philosophers term the 'illusion of reality' and reveal the nature of what lies beneath.

Towards The Collective: Tips for a better life

How do we attempt to live more fully; to experience the heady natural phenomena of the real? I would point readers towards Juan Mascaró's translation of *The Bhagavad Gita* and Sonya Richmond's 1969 guide, *Common Sense About Yoga*. Both describe ways to incorporate principles from ancient Indian thought into a life. Rupert Sheldrake ventured into similar territory (but from a western perspective) with his 2019 book, *Ways to go Beyond*. However, in the twenty twenties there may be a step which precedes the adoption of such practices. This is to first reduce the influence of the false collective in our lives. In theory, it should be simple. However, the unreal has become the water in which we swim to such an extent that it is important to learn to separate one's self from the surrounding societal landscape. It helps to understand that our way of life is not inevitable or universal, rather it is a deliberate construction, formed of philosophy, politics, and economics. This knowledge will help us see beyond the existing paradigm. Bear these ideas in mind, for in the following section, I attempt to describe ways in which we might disengage ourselves from the false collective.

If you are involved in music, then you may already be ahead of the game. While not a universal truth, communities which coalesce around music are often more attuned to the collective than mainstream society. The joint artistic endeavour of members of a band or other ensemble might be based upon collective communing in the shared unconscious. Perhaps this is the element which makes participating in music a special activity. However, it is not only bands that this applies to. Other forms of social music activity, such as DJ performances in clubs and festivals depend on a similar collective interplay. The artist is essentially sharing their love of music with the audience. Both feed each other via the collective and this creates the magic in the room. As any good DJ will testify, the audience matters. A good vibe is only possible when performer and crowd connect in a particular manner. The same can also be said of audiences at any performance in fact. Malcolm James details this effect in sociological terms, without overt reference to the collective unconscious in his 2020 book, *Sonic Impact*. However, his insightful analysis of music scenes that I have spent the best part of my life involved with, reveals a tacit acknowledgement of the universal mind or the true collective. These shared psychic phenomena fully explain the concepts of *vibe* and *sonic intimacy* which he refers to.

So be a musician, be a DJ, be into music. The communities which surround these activities, enjoy a close relationship with the true collective. Usefully, music remains a socially acceptable pastime in all strands of western society. A person can obscure their truer, higher ambitions behind the facade of simply having a good time, if that is necessary. In this way, one may appear to be a compliant, materialistic, neo-liberal capitalist when in reality the underlying motives are of a different nature entirely. Note, however, that all music scenes are not the same. There are some that are utterly prosaic, material, and shallow. Manufactured pop immediately comes to mind, but also consider the discussion in the earlier chapter *Paradoxes*. Remember, your friends might be your enemies and your enemies your friends. Discernment is key.

Even better than being involved in music is being spiritual. If you can commit to following a philosophy or theology such as yoga, this will stand you in good stead. Guiding principles of this nature will help you to remain on the path of good, regardless of the distractions or temptations. Beware, however, of dogmatism. This might be a false friend. Sonya Richmond stressed that an attitude of respect towards all theologies is healthy, but she also advised caution with regards to dogmatism. I fully concur with both aspects of this sentiment. Not everyone has the inclination to follow this path, which is fine. Wiser souls than I have pointed out that there are many routes up a mountain; varied in nature, but they all lead to the summit. In addition to music and theology, I suspect that the activities of many other communities tend towards the collective. These include sport, art, surfing, and mountaineering, but I am certain there will be others. Use that discernment described above to identify those which encourage genuine communing, rather than those which simply plug you into the plastic hive.

These notes regarding music and other scenes are rather generic, however. Therefore, more specific suggestions for distancing oneself from the false collective in the age of digital hegemony are presented in the following paragraphs. There is the palpable sense that the mass of humankind is losing the battle to maintain its humanity under the onslaught of technology. We are surrounded by input, continually distracting us, nudging us, deciding for us (it would seem) the things that we may want to do next. It is ubiquitous – the water in which we swim – so much so that there is a section of the population who have abandoned all thought of resistance, and now ape the machine. There are even extreme techno-futurists who seek to merge with it. There is a broad movement known as transhumanism, and within its boundaries there are those who see benefit in connecting the human nervous system to digital computers. In 2010 Jaron Lanier issued a warning to the world: 'you are not a gadget'. He predicted the widespread abdication of humanity to the digital paradigm. I hope that what follows is a small contribution to the counter offensive.

Rolling news is one of the most damaging aspects of modern media. If you find yourself plugged into rolling news, watching hollow-eyed as they repeat what you already know – ad-nauseam, then you are already dead, switch it off now. The only goal of media of this nature is to keep you attached to the teat of the false collective. Sitting there, watching blankly, you are depriving yourself of moments which could be spent communing with the transpersonal mind. Instead, you are engaging in no-value, purely addictive behaviour.

Entertainment offered on contemporary platforms may be more dubious than first imagined. Binging on anything is usually an indicator of unhealthiness. I remain unsure as to why society considers the *binge-watching* of drama series to be any different. Personally, I don't consume entertainment of this nature. Like rolling news, I consider it no-value behaviour. It keeps us attached to the device, the network, to the collective that isn't real. This, I hope, is not a puritan diatribe. I enjoy entertainment as much as the next person. However, I share Plato's suspicion of excessive consumption of drama. It is better perhaps to spend more time inhabiting the real – there is drama enough in that. However, as mentioned before, dogmatism is also unappealing – especially in myself. So once again, discernment is key. Perhaps readers with good knowledge of these genres can easily discern good from bad; offerings which encourage understanding of the true collective versus those that don't. I leave that final decision to you.

Music festivals have been discussed at length in the preceding paragraphs. I find that these are excellent environments in which to rehearse practices that encourage genuine communion. The reason for this is because in the words of Rachel Horne, festivals are 'spaces which break the rules of modern life'. This is precisely the objective of the suggestions in this section – to disrupt the norms, habits and rules that have us reaching for the device every few minutes. The following are tips for getting the most out of a music festival experience. You can also apply these to everyday life.

Leave the smartphone at home. Do not bring a smartphone to a festival. This is defeating the entire point of being at such an event. I sometimes bring an old 3G device if it is important that I am contactable, and even then, it is mostly left in my tent. Not having a smartphone means that I cannot take photographs or videos. The latter point has two benefits. Firstly, it means that I can only be in the moment, watching the performance and having a good time in the here and now. In her travel memoir, *Skating to Antarctica*, Jenny Diski wrote of tourists who were utterly engrossed in photographing the wildlife they encountered on the trip. She noted that they were in effect, living in the future – already imagining themselves back in their living rooms at home, proudly showing the videos and snaps to family and friends, and therefore bypassing the present moment entirely.

The second benefit of leaving the smartphone at home is that one doesn't then become party to what I term (with apologies to Noam Chomsky) *manufacturing discontent*. I use this expression for the effect of posting photographs and videos on social media which will feed the social comparison and fear which Byung-Chul Han wrote of. This leads to discontent in the lives of one's social media followers and therefore perpetuates the neo-liberal false collective. If we are seeking to break its power, we will need to cease manufacturing discontent. Therefore, no more posts of the nature of 'look at me! I'm having a wonderful time!' and the associated, unspoken subtext 'you are *so* missing out'.

While posts of this nature are also plain vulgar, we live in the age of vulgarity, so I am not so sure that anyone cares. Nonetheless, it is behaviour that is far removed from the true collective and much concerned with the illusion of hyper-individualism. Individualism of this form powers the neo-liberal carousel, and therefore takes us far from where we ultimately want to be. I reiterate the advice – leave your smartphone at home. Instead, invest your energy into engaging with the people around you at the festival – dancing, talking, or joking with strangers and – if you will excuse the hippy sentiment – sharing love. A smartphone is a burden in multiple ways. It is an attention stealer. The apps and notifications will distract you from the true collective communing that is likely to be happening right in front of you. It is also – literally – power hungry. You will find yourself spending another chunk of time worrying about how to keep it charged in order to continue engaging in the unhelpful behaviours described above.

Leave the smartphone at home.

A number of festivals now offer apps ('free download!') which contain the schedules as well as other features which ostensibly exist to allow audiences to 'get more' from the event. It is nothing less than neo-liberal creep. Resist this. Its only goal is to keep you tethered to the device and thus remain on the leash. Remember that the festival is a space for breaking the rules of modern life. Rule number one pertains to the smartphone. Break this norm. Leave it at home. Print out the schedule of acts before you leave. If you need to, store it in a waterproof holder in case of inclement weather. I have attended a festival (which shall remain nameless) that only listed the schedule on an app, and I did just that. I had a lot of fun floating around asking randomers which acts were on where. I also enjoyed making chance discoveries. Untethering, in this instance, was wonderful.

Leave the smartphone at home.

Connect with randomers. Aside from the smartphone, there are other behaviours that can help one to interact with the collective. These are practices which I rehearse annually at each festival I attend. One of the most important is that one should connect with strangers. Modern society encourages us to remain 'nuclear' – the nuclear family, the close group of friends etc. Build your nuclear, society says, then be wary of outsiders. This mode of modern life limits our ability to understand and experience the oneness of all. At festivals we can learn to break this particular rule of modern life. Be open to the people around you. Share smiles and a little conversation. Inspire other festival goers that you do not know by perhaps talking about the different performances that you have each seen. A considerable amount of magic can be the result of these fleeting interactions. When these communications occur, all parties are surprised by the fact that they are able to share in such an open manner. There were many such instances this summer, but I particularly remember a conversation with a septuagenarian Geordie. I was sat in front of a stage waiting for the next band to begin. I had – of course – no smartphone and I had already spent many hours studying the programme. So, I simply struck up conversation with the person sat next to me. This was not for any particular reason. He didn't appear especially interesting – it was just that he was sat nearby. We spent the next twenty-or-so minutes in wonderful conversation about Latin America and various genres of music. Neither of us was especially knowledgeable about the topics we discussed, but we both had enough of an opinion to make it a worthwhile interchange. Once the band started up, we said our goodbyes and melted into the audience. There have been many other similar moments at festivals I have attended over the years.

Spend time on your own. The little vignette above brings to mind another tip for helping to commune with the collective. That is, ensure that you spend time on your own. Be solitary in order to connect. These days I *prefer* being on my own at festivals. Even if I arrive with friends and we set up tents together, I will eventually excuse myself and head off unaccompanied. This is important because flying solo means that you can be attentive to the collective. One then has the cognitive space to process the things that are taking place around you. It means that you are free to choose the moments (and the performances) that you wish to experience. When I was younger, I, like many others, would share my festival experience with large groups of friends. This was fun but at some point, I realised that decisions regarding what to see and do were being made *en-masse*. The group would agree what should be done, and all would troupe off as a unit, each individual somehow being afraid of breaking off and doing something different. As I grew older, I remember wanting to be a part of various activities and performances that the group vetoed. It all changed for me one Saturday night when the group was heading back to where our tents were pitched. We passed what I considered to be an incredible party that was getting up to speed in one of the café tents. I suggested to the gang that we stop and explore the happening. A veto was issued. For the first time in my festival-going life, I broke away. I said 'you guys go back then. I'm going to stay here for a bit'. I was nervous and uncomfortable initially, but that discomfort soon passed, and I remained in that tent until the very early hours, dancing and exchanging moments with perfect strangers, communing with the great All. It was a memorable moment of realisation.

For sure, hang out with your friends, but some solitude is essential for one to find one's place in the collective. There is too much noise and not enough freedom in tightly bound groups. The pay-off is randomness. When randomness occurs and one is in a group, attention is usually focused on the group and the episode can easily pass you by. Alone, there is nowhere to hide from the phenomenon. One is forced to experience and process it. My next tip relates to this area.

Be open to randomness. The magic of the collective is ever present. It is happening around us constantly. We simply need to be open to it; to tune in. This is what Jung called synchronicity. The idea of synchronicity relates to coincidence, but not of the raw sort; rather it is *meaningful* coincidence. When distracted by the false collective, we belittle these moments of significance, considering them just a chance happening or some materialistic function of the brain. This, however, is what we have learned. It is the twenty-first century discourse: all is material, all is individual. Therefore, if one is too busy or distracted by technology and the mendacious collective, you might miss the display of universal alignment. If, however, you open yourself to the everything, you'll occasionally experience the odd awesome moment. These moments will leave you thinking 'that couldn't just have happened like that – could it?' for years to come. Synchronicity isn't only about the meaningful coincidence; it is about the subject recognising it as such. Therein lies the 'wow' moment. Being open to randomness allows this to happen.

Understand your inner shaman. A Lithuanian artist named Augustinas Našlėnas is responsible for this tip. I first met him in 2013 in his Sheffield studio which was located beneath the space that I was using as an office at that time. The route to the communal kitchen was via his studio and I would often stop and ask him questions about his work. One day he explained a piece in terms of shamanism. As is the case with newcomers to this topic, I had assumed this was an esoteric practice connected to tribal societies. Augustinas patiently explained aspects of these rituals, which I had not considered. Some of these were to do with being faithful to one's inner self and not being afraid of the (sometimes jarring) truths that one might encounter. Much like the *be open to randomness* tip above. Augustinas also spoke about Shamanism in terms of using one's specific abilities to inspire and help others.

I translated a few of these vague concepts into a loose mental framework through which to channel my behaviour at the next round of festivals that I was planning to attend. It transpired that during that summer I had especially rich and enjoyable interpersonal experiences. Simply put, I was more open and courageous. I was attuned to others, and honest regarding the communal drives within myself (to dance, to share) and therefore, I had a powerful feeling of contributing worthwhile moments to those gathered in the festival space. That is, I was one of the creators of the *vibe*. I found myself breaking many more of those rules of modern life. Obviously, I consumed alcohol and the odd spliff, but the positive outcomes were not wholly in my imagination. I can recall many excellent conversations that were shared and some of those very festival-specific, fleeting-yet-deep friendships. The measure of how much one is contributing needs to have some objective aspect, and not just be a purely subjective judgement.

These then are my suggestions for opening oneself to collective experiences. They are easy to practise in environments such as music festivals, and I would urge you to give it a try. There are many seasoned festival heads who already do these things. For those who are new to such practices, the rewards are considerable. However, the true purpose of this book is not to be a guide for festival goers. It is to attempt to describe an alternative to individualistic materialism; to sketch a modus operandi for the generation who are striving for something better than neo-liberal overload in the twenty-first century. Thus, these principles can also be applied away from music spaces, and within society itself. Doing so may foster a radical change in perspective. Of course, it is much easier to live in this way in the artificial environment of a music festival. For instance, much of everyday life and work is conducted on the Internet: banking, job -hunting, dating, and entertainment. Nevertheless, the goal should be only to use the smartphone and Internet when necessary and not to engage in mindless, addictive, and no-value behaviour. Being addicted is the tether that keeps you attached to the false collective. Make a habit of leaving your phone at home on at least a few occasions a week. You can purchase physical (paper) train tickets, use your bank cards for a change (or even cash!), and bring a book to read if you are going to be some place where boredom is likely.

Here are some other tips for removing yourself from the false collective in everyday life.

Notifications. Take some time to manage notifications on your phone. Essentially, switch them all off. This way you will look at apps when *you* want to, as opposed to being constantly jolted out of yourself by the incessant buzzing of the digital collar that is fastened metaphorically around your neck. If you are going to retain a few notifications, make them the ones associated with the real – calls, texts, and other messaging from people you love, not from some random online service telling you that there is fifty percent off summer shoes this weekend.

Digital nicotine. Do not install social media on your phone. Social media is the digital equivalent of nicotine. It keeps you coming back for more. If you have a computer at home, only use social media on that device. Do not take it everywhere you go. And that includes *Facebook/Meta/Instagram* and their associated messaging apps. These keep you plugged in. If you must, use a stand-alone messaging app on your phone (*Signal* or *Telegram* are great, *WhatsApp* at a push) and that is it. Try to avoid installing any messaging utility that is connected to a social media service on your phone.

Beware the bean. Be aware of the influence of coffee. Caffeine is powerful and useful if there is a task to complete and extra energy and focus are required. In my own life, there would have been many projects left unfinished were it not for the bean. However, caffeine causes one to become action-focussed and less inclined to drift around nebulously tapping into the collective. I don't drink coffee at festivals – I am always slightly amazed, watching the individuals who rise early and queue for coffee, which they drink while reading their favourite newspaper. I wish I were able to say to them 'Unplug! Commune! A festival is the perfect opportunity to do so'. In the same way that smartphones and social media are addictions, coffee is too. The worst aspect of these addictions is that if they are used mindlessly, they tend to pull one away from the collective. With this as our goal, we should think about our use of coffee. By all means, use it when there is a particular task to complete (long drive, heavy workload etc.). If we could stop drinking it when the thing is done, all would be well. However, coffee is incorporated into our lifestyle, and neo-liberal capitalists encourage it. We drink it on lazy Sunday mornings and at festivals when its effects prevent us from floating around in the All. Think.

Prune the feed. In this matter I am considering technology once again. We frequently sign up to online services and subsequently become a passive recipient of marketing material that the providers churn out. This fills your head with a stream of nefarious (and of course, false) narratives. Unsubscribe or cancel accounts as soon as these services show any sign of taking you for granted, or if the communications are of no value. Manage the accounts that you follow on social media. Be brutal. There may be someone that you initially followed for their hilarious cat videos. However, if their stream is now an invasive political discourse, then hit that unfriend/unfollow button. This is an unhappy collective, which takes you far from oneness and love.

Even do this for the things that you love. If the decisions that you make are being heavily influenced by your cherished social media feed, then prune that feed also. If you still want to make those choices, then you will anyway. If you do not, you will stop. The point is to remove yourself from the false community of chat, the nudging, the influencing, the mendacious 'we're all here together, caring for one another' when the reality is often a vendor-client relationship. If this point is unclear, I offer an example from my own life.

You will have gathered by now (I hope) that I am very enamoured of music. On particular social media platforms, I tend to follow festivals, venues, musicians, DJs and labels, both nationally and internationally. The marketing from these accounts previously left me feeling that I was missing out by not attending their events. There were a number of years where I felt that I attended too many events for this very reason. Some of these were functions I would not have been interested in, had it not been for my having been persuaded by relentless social media marketing. I have since unfollowed many accounts and find that those venues that I really wish to hang out at, I do. Those that are not so important to me fall by the wayside. When I am considering a night out, I look at the upcoming schedules of favourite spots. Pull instead of push. I am much freer to make my own decisions without the subliminal influencing.

It's about time. Time is an overarching battleground in the war between the true and the false collective. Of course, if we accept that the collective consciousness is an actual thing, then the *false* collective distracts us, it wastes our valuable waking life time with being concerned about no-value constructs; from extreme and emotional politics to the way in which one compares to others, and the clothes/vehicle/lifestyle choices that will allow us to rectify this. The world of the false collective will always exist, we will never banish it completely. What is different about contemporary existence (in comparison to previous epochs) is the way that the unreal demands our attention, from the moment we wake, to the moment when we fall asleep at night. The minimisation of smartphone and social media use are in part an attempt to claim back time for you; for that within which yearns to reach out to the great All. So even if you succeed in breaking a number of these digital habits, ensure that you use the freed time for activities which take you in the right direction. Read good books, be inspired by something, spend time in social groups which foster a sense of oneness. Where possible, try to step out of the nuclear modes of existence. Try to go beyond families and friends. The All is limitless, and you should be too.

Take control. By this I mean that we should be the opposite of automatic. Those mindless, no-value activities which we engage in – *doom scrolling* is the current parlance for online behaviour of this form – are problematic. The philosophy of *existentialism* would describe such behaviour as our being unwilling to take definite action. We are simply allowing the world to wash over us and are naïvely hoping that some good will come of it.

Existentialism is associated with the post-war Paris of cafés on the *rive gauche*, Jean-Paul Sartre, Albert Camus, and Simone de Beauvoir. It conjures up artsy individuals listening to jazz, smoking Gauloises, and passionately discussing life. The term itself is twentieth century but its roots can be traced back to two nineteenth-century giants of European philosophy: Soren Kierkegaard and Friedrich Nietzsche. Kierkegaard wrote that individuals had forgotten what it was to really exist; to live as if one's actions meant something. A century after Kierkegaard, Sartre and others took up these themes and existentialism was born. The four main strands of this philosophy are:

1. You are the result of your choices (not the opposite).

2. It's about time. The present, future and past are not the same; either in meaning or value.

3. The locus of existentialism is the human individual, and the search for meaning and identity.

4. Freedom to choose allows us to direct and change the direction in which our lives are heading at any given point in time.

What this means in respect of the collective is that we are required to *choose*, we have to *do*, we need to take definite, positive *action*. Passive doom scrolling (or any other automatic digital behaviour) is not this. It is letting someone else take control of your actions, of your thoughts. If you are not choosing, or acting, then the very definition of your self is subject to erosion. As Byung-Chul Han suggests, one optimises oneself to death. In a poem inspired by the words of Han, I once described this in another way: 'the nothing within seeks to connect to the nothing without'.

'Every day of one's life can be the beginning of great things'. So wrote Juan Mascaró in 1962, and his words capture the essence of the existential principles listed above. That which occurred yesterday is past. If one's previous actions produced a character that is perhaps sad, a little lost and thoroughly uninspired, then actions in the present can change that. If one chooses to act – consistently – in a new way, then the version of the person which emerges tomorrow might be quite different. The following is an example.

An individual may have been dreaming of a specific type of beautiful body which looks elegant in fashionable clothing. However, that same person has a recent history of mindless, automatic eating; that is, snacking on carbohydrate-rich foods. She doesn't stop to be mindful and therefore does not realise that each unhealthy morsel that she places in her mouth takes her dream further out of reach. That, however, is the existential past. Perhaps one day, or at one particular moment, she decides to adopt Mascaró's dictum and announces to herself that 'today will be my new beginning'. Armed with the Sartrean exhortation to *choose*, to be mindful, and to take control, every time she feels her arm (or mind) reaching towards the snack cupboard, she might implore her inner self to choose. 'If I do not eat the snack this time' she might say, 'and if I make the same choice every day from now on, then in three months' time I shall be a little more lithe, and a bit more buff'.

The goal of the true collective is the same. One arrives at the destination (mental health, joy, true connection) via taking back control of the behaviours that have been abdicated in favour of the false collective, of the digital paradigm. It may have been one's past for many years – sometimes since birth – but exercising this control is the first step towards great things. One foot in front of the other; keep your mind focused on the goal, and you will soon wake up in a future which is much brighter than the present. I urge you to do it. Of course, it will not be easy – habits and addictions are notoriously hard to break. However, the cliché *no pain, no gain* is appropriate here. Create a bonfire of the technological vanities!

The focus of this section has mainly been on areas that you are in control of, which, if we are being completely honest, is everything in your sphere of experience. This is because all is filtered through an individual's perception and will, and these two are areas which one is largely the master of. We have examined the smartphone, one's attitude to others, and being mindful and in control. How one uses the Internet was another area of focus. Nevertheless, in the midst of mindful rejection of the false collective, curveballs will appear. Neo-liberal capitalism is throwing them (and inventing new curveballs) constantly. Their aim remember, is to disrupt, and to prevent natural communion with the collective. While in the centre of Sheffield earlier today, I encountered one such curveball. Telephone boxes were once littered throughout our cities. These are now obsolete due to mobile communications technology. However, in some cases, the sites where these boxes once stood are being repurposed as eye-level, multimedia billboards. Some cities have them every few blocks. From the perspective of the false collective, this is a wonderful development. Even if a person is mindfully wandering through the city, having left their smartphone at home, they can still be assaulted by bold digital exhortations which disturb the individual's train of thought. Today it was a video advert for a news provider. There was a contentious, emotion-eliciting headline with associated video imagery. My instinctive reaction was to reach for my smartphone to find out more about the story. I paused for a moment and then thought 'Ah! They nearly got me'.

This example puts me in mind of a futuristic curveball, which Devin Coldewey recently described in Tech Crunch (Coldewey, 2022). The idea is that a high-resolution matrix of satellites would be launched into Earth orbit. Once in position they would be capable of producing points of light that are visible from the surface of our planet. The matrix could then be programmed to display marketing messages that would be visible in the night sky. This is disruption on a literally planetary scale. The overall point is that despite one's best efforts, there will always be unexpected distractions; attempts by the neo-liberal capitalists to erode your humanity in favour of the consumerist agenda. The existential tenets of freedom and choice – including of what one thinks – are important here, as is the exhortation to *take control*. Curveballs are a feature of life; they will always be encountered but it is our reaction to them which determines who we will be in the future. For our purposes, we should experience them and not react. Turn away, do not (mentally) engage. Walk, as Dionne Warwick once sang, on by – literally as well as metaphorically.

If I make fortunes from what I do, then I have failed. Or neo-liberalism, the digital paradigm, and the path of the real. In our contemporary western societies, it is important to have enough money to live. This is especially the case in the digitally enabled, neo-liberal (c)age. There is a part of my thinking that would quite like to channel Lennon and McCartney and declare that 'money can't buy me love'. However, I have lived long enough to know that for the ordinary citizen, such sentiments are fanciful. Perhaps you are in the enviable position where you can live off-grid, you grow your own food, and are totally self-sufficient. This is rare. Most of us need an income. Nevertheless, when it comes to money, like the slow addiction to caffeine touched upon earlier, it is good to be wary of the semi-conscious slip from making money to survive, to becoming overly enamoured of the rewards of individualistic neo-liberal capitalism. Earning a living is a gateway drug to neo-liberal capitalism. The former is perfectly fine. Having a fulfilling career in which the remuneration is such that one can exist in a comfortable manner is, of course, uncontroversial. Moreover, there are those who in their work, entertain admirable thoughts of changing the world with innovations – even digital ones – which might improve the lives of others in society. However, once on that path, the urge to monetize should be resisted if one is not to contribute to, and become part of, the false collective. That urge for multi-digit growth; the dream of making a fortune – such is the slow descent towards separating oneself from the collective.

For example, let us imagine that one day, the ideas I am outlining on these pages come to the attention of neo-liberals, who detect in them an opportunity for profit. I dearly hope that this is not the case, but it is not outside the realms of possibility. For instance, consider black music – a form once ridiculed by mainstream white society when it was post-slavery music. Capitalism has no shame, however, and the pop music industry, which developed via the exploitation of Afro-diasporic forms, is testament to that fact. Neo-liberal capitalism would do the same to these writings if it could devise a method of monetizing these ideas. If that were to occur and the siren song of material wealth were sung to me, I would need to ask myself an existential question. Am I willing to forgo principles and seek to become inordinately wealthy, probably at the expense of my fellow citizen? Or would I do the right thing and act in accordance with the morals that ennoble me, and not with greed? Perhaps it is possible to be wealthy and retain one's principles. However, I suspect that it is very difficult and that such individuals are rare. If you think that you can do it, you probably cannot. Any logic aimed at convincing yourself that you can, is likely to be an unconscious attempt at self-deception. Neo-liberal capitalist materialism is infectious. Once a single toe is dipped in the pool, the entire body becomes infected. In the inimitable language of Guy Debord in *Society of the Spectacle*:

> The alienation of the spectator to the profit of the contemplated object … is expressed in the following way: the more he contemplates the less he lives; the more he accepts recognizing himself in the dominant images of need, less he understands his own existence and his own desires (Debord, [30]).

Stay away from the pool. Thus, if you find that I have made a fortune from these ideas, this will mean that I have failed.

A Short History of Tech

Digital technology is a contemporary enabler of the false collective, but in truth, the discourse of the unreal existed long before the web, computers, or even the transistor came into being. Marshall McLuhan in *The Medium is the Massage*, suggested that the creation of a technology as humble as the alphabet altered humans and their subsequent ideas of themselves. He also declared that 'print technologies created the mass' (as in *the masses*). McLuhan was writing in the nineteen sixties, when the vanguard of technology was the transistor, and the application which was shaping society at that point was the television (paradoxically created using earlier vacuum tube technology). McLuhan's theories suggest that the false collective is not dependent on any specific technology. One could argue that certain sections of society have always sought to dominate, control, and distract others. Individuals or groups thus motivated might make use of whatever communication technology is available to further their ends. Or perhaps it is us; perhaps it is our weaknesses – ourselves when the lake surface is agitated – who invoke this false narrative and perpetuate it via the means that are to hand in any given epoch.

The Medium Is the Massage was published in the same year as Guy Debord's *Society of the Spectacle* (1967) and at times the two books complement each other. Debord explains that which underlies the social effects of media (which he terms *spectacle*) thus:

> The oldest social specialization, the specialization of power, is at the root of the spectacle (Debord [23]).

It is power relations then, which Debord argues that are at the heart of the false collective. He explores this in greater depth.

> The fetishistic, purely objective appearance of spectacular relations conceals the fact that they are relations among men and classes: a second nature with its total laws seem to dominate our environment. But the spectacle is not the necessary product of technical development. The society of the spectacle is on the contrary the form which chooses its own technical content. If the spectacle, taken in the limited sense of 'mass media' which are its most glaring superficial manifestation seems to invade society as mere equipment, this equipment is in no way neutral but is the very means suited to its total self-movement.

As with the nature of electronic equipment of the nineteen sixties, so too the technologies of the digital age. It is naïvely assumed that the dangers of contemporary tech are due to the properties of the platforms themselves. For example, 'the Internet can be harmful to children and those with suicidal thoughts' or 'social media can be dangerous to vulnerable people due to online bullying'. There is a misunderstanding at the heart of such opinion. It is not social media per se that is problematic. Social media, as with all digital technology, is a reflection of the political and economic philosophy under which it was created. Indeed, as will be outlined in the following paragraphs, the innovators, who created many of the personal computing concepts that our digital world is predicated upon, were utopians and counter-culturalists. It is interesting to note the way in which their inventions – designed to support high ideals – were co-opted for completely contrary purposes.

I encountered a powerful example of this process in the recent documentary *Money Bots*. At the end of the film the trading algorithm designer turned whistle-blower, Haim Bodeck, reflected upon his journey from idealist to enabler of the unreal:

> When I got into this business, I thought the whole point was to replace the old boys club, to get rid of it. What I learned after twenty years is ... what we ended up doing was that we automated the old boys club. It's alive, it's thriving, it's in the algos.

The words of Haim Bodeck might be a suitable epitaph to the high ideals of those who first envisaged, then created the personal computing paradigm in the 1960s and 1970s. As is the way of innovations that wind up being exploited by the forces of capitalism, the idea was unpopular with the mainstream during the decade of its birth. This may be surprising to contemporary readers for whom personal computing *is* computing. However, back then the smart money was in corporate and military computing and that meant the mainframe. IBM bestrode this market segment in colossus fashion, and the other big players attempted to play catch up, for example: ICL, DEC, and Sperry Univac. The dominant line of thought then was 'who wants a *personal* computer? What would an individual do with one?' What made sense at that time was computers as massive number crunching devices which sat in cooled data centres in office basements. Programs were loaded on punch card or tape (and in the latter years, floppy disk) and they whirred away, processing finance numbers, sales figures, HR data, and salaries. The early part of my technology career was spent in such environments, and even though the personal computer revolution had already started, the majority of large enterprises had yet to embrace the change.

At this point, a definition of the term 'personal computing' might be helpful. This was not a reference to particular hardware, rather it referred to the use that the technology might be put to. The computer devices themselves were classified as either *mainframe*, *mini*, or *micro*. Indeed, in its early years the now giant Microsoft included a hyphen in its name 'Micro-Soft' to indicate that it produced software for micro computers. Personal computing and its origins as a paradigm can be located in the early nineteen sixties. Various thinkers, notably Doug Engelbart, authored papers which explored the use of computers as devices to augment human cognition. This would necessitate real-time operation of the technology. At this point in history the number-crunching mainframes were operated in *batch mode*. That is, commands and data were fed in advance to the device and scheduled to run at a future time. The results were collected once this process was complete. The goal of real time methods of operating computers was to allow interaction between person and device and therefore, achieve the cognition-aiding goals of Engelbart and others. Another influential contributor to the idea of personal computing was Stewart Brand, who gave voice to elements of U.S. West coast counter-cultural thought. He suggested that information technologies should be used for democratic and decentralising purposes. In respect of this, information sharing was key to his design. The personal computing paradigm, Brand suggested, should incorporate the ability for computers to communicate with one another.

Thus, in these design goals, we find the most important elements of the personal digital technologies which surround us today. Small, personal devices employing human-centred interface methods (today we have touch and even voice control) and importantly, interconnectivity. The early pioneers thought that computing of this nature could be used for good. For example, the power of personal computers might be used as intelligence or memory aids: the to-do list, the calendar with reminder notifications, language translation facilities; the calculator. Furthermore, Internet working held the promise of wide sharing of information as well as the ability to connect like-minded individuals.

Personal computing as a concept was initially ignored by the capitalists. The first such device, the *Palo Alto* funded by Xerox, was demonstrated to executives in nineteen seventies. John Markoff, in his excellent *What the Dormouse Said*, argued that as far back as 1977 the Xerox executives had in their exclusive grasp a new technology that was about to change the world and they failed to recognise the fact. They were subsequently accused of fumbling a once in-an-epoch opportunity. In 1979, so the story goes, a young Steve Jobs visited the Xerox Palo Alto research centre (PARC), saw this personal computing device, and returned home with the idea of the graphical user interface. Jobs subsequently designed the Apple Macintosh II computer.

Even in 1990, a decade or so on from this point, personal computers were not yet mainstream. Certainly, in many enterprises, there was a networked P.C. on each desk, and creatives were using Apple Macs to design products, magazines, music, and the like. Gaming on microcomputers was already a growing and popular segment. However, the mass adoption event for personal computing, was the World Wide Web. I was first shown it by a French PhD student in Oxford during the summer of 1994 and realised that it would change everything. And it did. By the autumn of that year, I'd created my first web page *Brighton Clubland* on the University of Sussex computers. The early World Wide Web (web 1.0) in large part fulfilled the visions of the Californian dreamers. It enhanced our cognitive abilities, by allowing us to search a massive database (the Internet) and it brought us together. The early collaborations, forums and social interactions were often friendly and polite. It was a system which allowed us to commune with strangers. The false collective only seriously realised the potential of personal computing in the years surrounding the millennium. The dotcom boom of 2000 was a super indicator that big money sought to lay its grubby paws on this new digital paradigm. However, web 1.0 still reflected its counter-cultural origins of its creators. It was designed for sharing, and knowledge enhancement.

In 2010 Jaron Lanier wrote 'something started to go wrong with the digital revolution around the turn of the twenty-first century. The world wide web was flooded by a torrent of petty designs sometimes called web 2.0' (Lanier, p. 3). In whatever way the technical folk might opt to describe it, web 2.0 transformed the web from being that sharing, knowledge-enhancing, and community-forming technology to one that automated individualist, neo-liberal capitalist materialism. Ease-of-use (or the 'comfort' in Tara Brabazon's aphorism) is a signpost of the presence of neo-liberalism: VIP lanes, hands-free boot opening, wheelie suitcases, out-of-town and car-friendly hypermarkets. They lure you with comfort and then drop the cookie which subsequently disrupts your life. I once attempted to describe this poetically.

Don't Go Digital

Don't go digital
People of the world.

Digital is a Venus fly trap
An angler fish
The gossamer silk of the black widow.

Why would you want to discard
Paper and ink and vinyl
Or even flesh and blood
For pixelated promises of a better tomorrow.

They tempt you with comfort, with ease-of-use
With the ability to do that only imagined in dreams.

The cheese on the trap.

They seek to harvest your soul
To manipulate your meaning
To track and measure and crunch you
To their own avaricious ends.

They seek not a better tomorrow for your sweet soul
No, your discarded material husk will be testament to that fact
When they are done with you.

Beware this melody known well to sirens

Dance around the off and on,
The black and white
The zero and one
Dance as only you, ineffable analogue child

Of infinity and cosmic dust,
Can.

No, don't go digital
Stay as lovely and human as you are.

Even though web 2.0 is the bad guy, I wish that web 1.0 had not happened. Web 1.0 sucked me in. Here is a medium, I thought, that allows me to connect to others around the world. I had wonderful conversations with interesting individuals and was sent digital music tracks from artists located in faraway countries. I discovered new stuff; for instance, Danish chillout, and a proto-social media website called *Flork* – the purpose of which was to serve up a random profile of another user. If you liked what you read, you could send them a brief note and occasionally quite interesting correspondences would ensue. There were also the chat rooms and forums – often polite and community centric.

In 2003 *SheffieldForum.co.uk* helped me to orient myself and make real-life contacts upon my arrival in the steel city. Prior to that, in the late nineteen nineties I created a poetry webzine (hand-coded in HTML and later PHP) just for the love of the art form – it was neither commercialised nor monetized. A group of the UK poets coalesced, and we organised in-person events in London, were invited to perform at a music festival, and some of those with whom I collaborated on this project remain my best friends to this very day. None of this would have been possible without web 1.0. Nevertheless, the original WWW prepared the ground for our acceptance of web 2.0. The later version appeared similar to the earlier one, but it was in fact very different. We only discovered this when it was much too late – when all of society was suckered into carrying a smartphone everywhere, banking digitally, and accepting the move of human-centred services to digitally-automated ones. This was labelled progress, and it often employed the mendacious prefix *smart*, but from the perspective of the citizen, of the member of the public, neither was wholly true. These developments were certainly progress for the neo-liberal class because it tethered us to their discourse; to their false collective, and as time goes by there are seemingly fewer avenues through which to escape from the digital cage.

Web 2.0 is about power and money. It does not enable communication between equal entities. It invests power in the larger instances and thus we, the regular users, are required to submit to their technological might. It is digital serfdom masquerading as freedom and brings to mind the seventeenth century words of Jean-Jacques Rousseau:

Il n'y a point d'assujettissement si parfait que celui qui garde l'apparence de la liberté ; on captive ainsi la volonté même.

There is no subjection so complete as that which preserves the forms of freedom; it is thus that the will itself is taken captive - Rousseau (1762/1993; p. 100).

And this serfdom is becoming embedded in the very structure of the way in which we live today. The purpose of life, the overriding reality in the view of Kastrup and Indian philosophy is the collective, the transpersonal mentation, Brahman, the All. However, we are prevented from reaching towards this by the activity of the false collective. The false collective has always existed, but formerly we knew of places in which we could escape its influence and commune in peace. Digital technology seeks out those hiding places and eradicates them in the name of power and profit.

Having said all of that, material reality is what it is. We need to eat; most of us have a need for a reasonable level of comfort. Thus, we will find the Internet useful. Knowledge of the true nature of the web will help us to use it wisely, however. Using browser extensions and ad blockers are two examples of this, and most of all, being mindful of what you are doing – and why – is useful.

If this section feels polemical, it is. I can make no apologies for being passionate regarding the present direction of travel. The idea of watching societies which have fought hard for citizen freedoms, sleepwalk into a new serfdom is reason enough for passion. Here, however, I leave my fiery distaste for these aspects of web 2.0 and return to other things that we might do with our free time once we have liberated (at least some of) it from the tyranny of the technological false collective.

What Is *Social* Anyway?

We use the word *social* in an individualist-materialist sense. In everyday usage it refers to the physical process of bringing individuals into proximity with one another and the subsequent communication which ensues. As described in the earlier part of this text, much of contemporary existence is viewed through the lens of a physicalist philosophy. *Social* interpreted in this way is simply proximity and data. Psychologists discuss the affective content of social interactions, while graph theory allows analysis of the properties of actors who occupy particular positions in the social network. Naturally, this is all very materialistic and a little deterministic too. The deeper nature of *social* is often left unexplored. Biologists and psychologists tend to offer the explanation that humans are genetically or biologically programmed to seek social interaction. This is one of those a-priori explanations, which mavericks such as Kastrup, Sheldrake, and even Ralph Nagel in his 2014 text *Mind and Cosmos*, regard with suspicion. They view these conclusions as incomplete or even incorrect.

Thus, if we are suspicious of the materialist fob-off of 'genetically inclined', what then is *social* really? I believe that ideas about the collective offer some insight. Social is the golden thread, it is our innate tendency to reconnect to the All. It is Wordsworth's youth in search of the light in *Intimations of Immortality*. Social isn't just an incidental feature of being human, it is the most important aspect! It is our seeking to commune with the unity of the collective. I find some support for this notion in Indian philosophy. This tradition describes multiple paths to ascend the mountain of life. One of these, *Bhakti* is what we in the west would describe as religious devotion and service. Another, *Jnana*, is elevation via learning and reason – philosophy and thought. *Raja* is a process which operates via meditation. Finally, there is *Karma* which does not mean 'fate', as is often mistakenly thought. Rather Karma is action. It is very similar to the existential idea of actions in the present having the power to change who one might be in the future. It is also very social. In the words of Sonya Richmond:

> With other Yogas one can be shut away in a room by oneself and study or concentrate or meditate in peace and silence. Not so with Karma Yoga. To practise it you need other people (Richmond, 1972; p. 115).

To my mind, social is the little-understood process of communing with the collective. It is inherently spiritual and more so if one makes it so. Social is not limited to humans of course. Ants and bees are famously social animals. The *reason* for their social behaviour remains a mystery to science aside from the usual biological explanation of reproduction; that is, to raise the next generation. However, if we are seeking a framework that is as true for humans as it is for ants, then it must explain why non-reproductive social relationships exist among unrelated individuals in human societies.

Seirian Sumner's wonderful scholarship describes the way in which ants and bees have evolved from the wasp. The wasp is the proto-social insect. If these creatures are also guided by a process similar to the morphic resonance (communicating with some supra-individual consciousness) which Rupert Sheldrake describes, then such an explanation of *social* can be shared between insects and humans. It is especially useful that the collective can also describe the aetiology of social behaviour of humans in situations where there is no genetic payback. Thus, the various contexts above can share a single explanatory hypothesis – that the mysterious collective is what draws beings together. An added bonus of this notion is that it would also shine an unfavourable light upon the techno-futurist term *hive mind*. In terms of the collective, bee hives are an occasion for organic communication with a transpersonal mentation. The artificial, so-called hive mind imagined by the digital technologists, may well be emergent, but it is also a materialistic, proximal method of communication and is guided by deterministic algorithms with a particular neo-liberal end in mind.

To sum up then, we use the term *social* casually, materialistically, perhaps not realising the central role that human-to-human interaction plays in the totality of things. Each time an alter communicates with another alter (to use the language of Kastrup), it is an opportunity to bridge the dissociative boundary (at least temporarily), which is why interactions of a deeper nature are so profound.

> You know, when we communicate with one another, and we feel that we have connected, and we think that we're understood, I think we have a feeling of almost spiritual communion. And that feeling might be transient, but I think it's what we live for. (Kim Krizan, Waking Life, 2001).

The Society of Listeners and Lovers

Byung-Chul Han's highly recommended volume *The Expulsion of the Other* is a meditation on the relationship between the *self* and the *other*. The argument is made that in the consumerist west, the true nature of otherness is being erased. This is because the other, like all else in society, must be commoditised. In order for this to happen, its rough edges are smoothed. It is made palatable and marketable. By the end of this process the other is expunged; it turns into that which Han terms the *selfsame*. Herein lies a problem – the other defines the self via its strangeness, and so in order not to erase ourselves along with the other, we must learn to co-exist with it. *The Expulsion of the Other* is a fascinating essay and has been a significant influence on this one. The author devotes a chapter at the end to listening. He offers the suggestion that through listening, we learn to cross (but not obliterate) the chasm between self and other. We do this through love and sparking the real communication that Kim Krizan spoke of in the *Waking Life* quote which ended the previous section.

It is useful then that Han effectively outlines a method through which we can transmit love along the golden thread because outside of nuclear relationships, I would hazard a guess that most do not know how to begin. How do we share love with strangers (or *others* in Han's terminology)? I have discussed the music festival at length, but such events are only occasional. The goal is to take such an attitude into everyday life. Performed correctly, listening is a subtle yet powerful method. As Han explains – and this is yet another example of paradox – listening can either be a vehicle for true communing with others, or it may simply be a shallow, material act. Listening of the useful variety is not passive, Han tells us. He describes the stages of listening: welcoming the other, then gifting one's ear to the other. The silence of the listener is the friendship. It is love. In such a listening, the other has an opportunity to speak themselves free.

In the Korean-German professor's description of listening I detect an ideal model of sociability. We all have experienced deep connection in nuclear settings or perhaps with randomers. These often become idealised moments, shimmering memorials to friendships and relationships that are remembered always. What each listener does is to ennoble the other and then in different scenarios, the listeners will themselves become *others* in their turn. Thus, the cycle of sharing propagates. Indeed, if Hanian listening was more widely practised, perhaps the world would be a little more wonderful. It is also a practical method through which we can learn to commune collectively. Han suggests that the digital paradigm prevents true listening due to the restricted nature of the responses that platforms make available to us. Examples of this are 'like' and 'reply'. Therefore, online interactions are less likely to be useful in this regard. It is best to practise true listening in non-digital spaces.

I cannot of course suggest that you accost unknown strangers and demand conversation. This might occasionally be tolerated in friendly Sheffield, but it might inspire all manner of abuse in a larger city like London. On a more serious note, there are always numerous opportunities, every day, to interact kindly with others: commuting, hanging out in cafés, or even at the supermarket. In our busy societies interactions occur frequently. It is our choice whether we continue to treat these as transactions or make the attempt to embrace the others on a deeper, more human basis. Above and beyond this, remember that thought is key. There are many philosophical and theological aphorisms of the nature of 'as you think, so you become'. The underlying idea is that thoughts are actions too. The existential tenet that actions in the present determine the future, holds true for thoughts also. If one wanders through this life with a head filled with ugly thoughts, chances are that the future of that person will tend towards ugliness too, regardless of what they attempt to project for the sake of appearances. Thoughts then, are key. Byung-Chul Han's listening is primarily a thought exercise. Nothing is said or done. One simply thinks kindly of the other, listens to what they are saying and resolves not to interrupt. One can act kindly or unkindly. The same is true with thought. With absolutely zero verbal or physical interaction with another person, an act of love or hate can be performed. One can feel kindness or affection for the other that one is regarding. One can also think unkindly of them. Each option is a step on a path to differing tomorrows.

What Cannot Be Spoken

Last night I was pondering Kastrup's notion that metabolising entities are dissociated alters of a transpersonal mentation. In other words, there is a single universal mind that our consciousnesses are all a part of. According to this theory, we are separated by dissociative boundaries which means that I cannot know your thoughts, nor you mine. A feature of the theory which I have attempted to construct in this volume, is that love may be the ingredient which dissolves the boundaries to some extent. Once this has occurred, we can then access what Sheldrake and Jung describe as the collective unconscious. Jung thought that archetypes (patterns of behaviour which recur across human societies) are manifestations of this shared psyche. The appearance of these and alternatively, the way in which living things are influenced by morphic resonance, are (in Kastrupian terms) simply the crossing of dissociative boundaries and accessing the cloud of psychic stuff shared with those we are related to. During these musings, I considered the way in which children are able to form loving relationships more easily than adults. We rather cynically put it down to naivety, innocence and biology, but it may be that their newly created alters have boundaries that are a little less established and more porous than adults. In other words, perhaps it is much easier for children to practise the communing and collectivity described throughout this volume than adults. It might even explain why on rare occasions young children have been known to seemingly access memories of previous lives – an effect which apparently fades as they age. This eerie phenomenon known as *past-life memory* is described in a paper published by Jim Tucker in 2008.

However, the analytic idealism of Bernardo Kastrup is but one manner of describing the real. All of these descriptions: Kastrup, Jung, Sheldrake, The Bhagavad Gita, psychonauts, near death experiences are simply words and models to describe an ontology which in truth may be beyond words. Ancient Indian thought recognises this. In the Upanishads we find the verse 'What cannot be spoken with words, but that whereby words are spoken: know that alone to be Brahman (Kena Upanishad, Part I; in *The Upanishads* translated by Juan Mascaró, 1965). To an extent, Kastrup understands this also. Words are representations of phenomena which are not wordy. The word *blue* is not the colour blue. A contemporary philosopher named Hilary Lawson identifies this paradox via his concept of *closure*. According to Lawson, the real world is unknowable stuff. Using our words, concepts, and mental schemata, we 'close' this nebulous goo into specific elements: a table, a chair, an alter, a boundary. The stuff remains nebulous, we simply overlay a mental structure upon it.

The dissociated alters and transpersonal mentation of Kastrup may simply be Sheldrake's local and remote consciousnesses, or Freud's personal versus Jung's collective unconscious. Indeed, these might be equivalent to the Vedantic Atman in relation to Brahman. Furthermore, the Rastafarian *I and I* or the African *Ubuntu* may be alternative descriptions of the universal All. We even find these concepts in the reports of near-death and psychedelic experiences, except once again described in varied language.

Near Death

In recent years a substantial number of near-death experience reports have been published both in academic journals (see for example, the Sam Parnia paper *Death and consciousness*) and on specialist websites such as *NDERF.org*. The ubiquity of these reports suggests that NDEs have probably always been a feature of human history. These events illuminate, I think, the shaky ground upon which the materially situated world view rests. Prior to the recent study of this phenomenon, reaction to accounts of post-mortal cognition was mainly incredulity; it was often suggested that they were the result of hallucination. Indeed, as recently as 2010, I had a (now deleted) online discussion with the *Psychology Today* editor Christian Jarrett who argued that the self-reports of NDE subjects might be unreliable. I was amused that a psychologist, hailing from a discipline in which the self-report questionnaire is the basis for a vast number of published studies, would respond in this way.

I first encountered the phenomenon in Raymond Moody's seminal publication *Life After Life*, which for some reason was on a bookshelf at my family home. After reading it, my own reaction was also tinged with incredulity. This response was, I suppose, caused by the dissonance between my western upbringing (moderated a little by the Caribbean culture of my home environment) and the challenging information I was encountering in *Life After Life*. Moody was the first to bestow respectability on this topic. He was a physician, a respected practitioner of materialist science. The book recounted patient experiences which were completely at odds with the prevailing scientific orthodoxy. Thomas Kuhn would term phenomena such as the ability of resuscitated patients to describe events and conversations that took place while they were clinically dead as *paradigmatic anomalies*. My other reaction to the book was hope. The maverick in me was quite pleased that these reports shook the hubris of materialistic science. Furthermore, these anomalies resonated with a hunch that lurked deep within me: this is not all there is.

Of course, the simple feeling that there is 'something more' is hardly the basis for a hypothesis – especially without further evidence. Although, if scientific researchers are brutally honest with themselves and us, I think that they might admit that it is often an emotion or intuition which is the seed of many a theory. Brute facts to the contrary will of course obliterate such subjective feeling and emotion, but where one of these intuited hypotheses is supported, it can herald the beginning of a research passion. It certainly was this way with NDEs and me.

The Internet, much maligned in various parts of this text, has enabled the collection of NDE reports from across the globe (paradox again). The self-reports contained on *NDERF.org* (pleasingly coded in a web 1.0 style) are littered with consistent themes that are also found in the academic work of Raymond Moody, Sam Parnia, Pim van Lommel, and others. NDEs appear to be of two types, positive and negative. The former greatly outweigh the latter. Features of a positive NDE include an experience of being out of one's body immediately after death. At this stage, a near death experiencer is often able to observe events occurring near to the body that they have just vacated. In many cases, reports of this nature have been corroborated by medics and others who were in the room at the time. The subject often hears a ringing sound, and sometimes travels through a tunnel or crosses some sort of threshold. Many report arriving in a beautiful environment (for example, a meadow), meeting deceased relatives and other knowledgeable beings. Another frequently reported feature is the life review. Finally, NDEs often end with the subject being told that they need to return to their body as there is 'work to complete'. Subjects subsequently find themselves back in their everyday state of being. In recalling their NDEs, those who have experienced the post-mortal state frequently report the sensation of being connected to all living things.

Science has struggled to establish a coherent narrative to explain NDEs. The phenomenon challenges many tenets of the current paradigm, especially with regard to consciousness. The materialist consensus has coalesced around the idea that NDEs are the last, fantastical activity of a dying brain. The reason that science has found itself trapped in this explanation is that materialism, by its very nature, cannot accept that there can be a mind without a (material) brain. It is a fascinating debate, which readers should explore for themselves. Kastrup's 2014 volume, *Why Materialism Is Baloney* might be a useful starting point. To the experiencers themselves these debates are often superfluous as their NDEs are to them, the most profound experiences of their lives and are frequently the catalyst for major life changes.

Other hints of the existence of a mysterious transpersonal mentation are much more quotidian. They include dreams and (serious) mental illness.

The understanding of dreams that has been gained from scientific research is useful from a mechanical perspective. For example, it has demonstrated that dreaming occurs during a phase of sleep known as rapid eye movement (REM). However, beyond this, research has only thrown a very limited light on the way in which dreams relate to consciousness itself. There is a mystery here which materialistic science refuses to engage open-mindedly with. Gary Lachman's discussion of pre-cognitive dreams discussed earlier, suggests that dreaming is a symptom of a far more complex reality than the one which we casually experience. His attempts at explanation incorporate musings on the nature of time as well as consciousness. Sadly, a fuller examination of these topics is certainly beyond the scope of this book – perhaps in the next one! The point to keep in mind is that there may be something else at play beyond the prosaic materialism that we are continually presented with. This alternative may have a feature – the collective unconscious, the golden thread. It matters not which metaphor one chooses (or the angle one wishes to view it from); the concept suggests a hidden process of communication between us all which is organic and natural and as yet unexplained by our materialist philosophy.

Sugar

Look, try not to be suckered by the arrogance of the scientific discourse. All current theories are correct – until they are shown to be otherwise. This is the fate of all such knowledge (therefore, be a philosopher). Newtonian science was once as proud and as assured of its veracity as its contemporary equivalent. There were even commentators at the end of the nineteenth century who boasted that all that was needed were some measurement improvements and the paradigm of classical physics would be able to explain everything. Shortly afterwards, as discussed previously, Einstein, and then the quantum researchers revealed the utter hubris of that statement.

Quantum mechanics is mysterious. Those familiar with it are aware of the spooky nature of certain effects. These are as yet unexplained, although they are reliable. I view them as the open door through which we walk into the room occupied by Kastrup, Sheldrake, and Jung, and will ultimately lead us to that which the Indian sages described thousands of years ago. You may choose to wait for contemporary science to arrive at this point before changing your behaviour. However, remember that science may not be able to unlock the secrets of the human soul. Here philosophers such as the existentialists are useful, as are the mavericks who have your best interests at heart, for example, Rupert Sheldrake. Then there are the spiritual specialists who do not wait for scientists to confirm the truths that they ascertain, for these are truths of consciousness, and of the psyche; the spirit, the soul. The current paradigm is yet to accept that any of these exist, which is fine. Science is as science does. Launching the scientific revolution in the sixteenth century, Francis Bacon (inspired by the Spanish inquisition no less) devised a methodology described by Professor Steve Fuller as 'torturing' the material world via experimentation to force it to reveal its secrets. The spirit is much harder to capture, to lock in a laboratory, and far less to torture. Therefore, if you wish to only live according to the tenets of science, then you might need to dispense with your existing notion of love and simply deal in a world of epiphenomena instead. Personally, I would suggest that we use science for what it excels at – understanding the relationship between material things, and not to expect any stunning insights into our inner lives. Note that this is not a dualist position, consciousness and material *are* made of the same stuff. However, I am with Kastrup, I do not subscribe to the view that material is primary, and consciousness emanates from it, rather consciousness is primary, and material is a part of the universal mentation. It is material which is the epiphenomenon.

I am approaching the end of this treatise. I hope that it has offered readers new ways in which to regard the world. Via this alternative viewpoint it may be possible to devise methods to escape the cage of the false collective. The cage then, is mental. It is learned helplessness; a sense of being overwhelmed. It is the cognitive state of permanent distraction; alerts and notifications which do not allow the within to settle upon a fruitful and beneficial train of thought. It is the agitation of negative states like pride, envy, anger, and greed which, as the Vedantic texts suggest 'lead to destruction'. The false collective takes us here. Do not be the late summer wasp – be a bee. Live in harmony with the *real* hive mind, not an over-hyped, plastic facsimile. We certainly do not understand the workings of this collective, but over millennia and across cultures we have been offered many clues about its worth. Once a toe is dipped in the waters of the All, and the positive returns are experienced, such behaviour becomes contagious. One will always seek to return to that – shall we say – joy, because there are no other experiences which ring so deeply true and satisfying. Give it a go.

The contagious aspect of the real puts me in mind of many aphorisms from Indian thought but also, obliquely, of Roald Dahl's work, *The Story of Henry Sugar*. This is a tale of a very wealthy man who lives selfishly and avariciously – a caricature of those of a certain class and ilk. In the story, he finds himself playing cards with rich friends in a grand house one evening. The game required an equal number of players and in this instance, there was one too many so, after drawing lots, Henry was ejected from the table. Frustrated, he wandered aimlessly around the house and found himself in the library where he idly picked up a book about an Indian Yogi who learned to see without using his eyes (note: this is fiction).

Following his reading of the short book Henry, motivated by greed of course, realises that such a skill would make him unbeatable at casino card games, and foreseeing an opportunity to increase his wealth, he sets out to learn how to meditate and to develop this special power.

Soon, amazingly (fiction, remember), he begins to acquire the skill. He rushes to the nearest casino, and because he is able to see through the cards to the other side, he leaves with a considerable sum of money. Initially, he celebrates, but shortly afterwards, our protagonist experiences a feeling of shallowness. Eventually, he comes to the realisation that the intense period of meditation required to gain this wondrous skill had somehow elevated his consciousness. Greed was now abhorrent to him. For Henry Sugar, a contagion occurred once he had dipped his toe into the pool of the All. The story concludes with the death of Henry, having become a major philanthropist who founded charities around the world. I hope that the non-fantastical elements of Henry's story are your story.

If such contagion exists, why do societies continue to promote the discourse of the false collective in seemingly ever larger numbers? Earlier, I suggested that perhaps negative emotions, such as greed and the lust-for-power, were at the heart of it. However, Carl Jung in *The Archetypes and the Collective Unconscious* volume suggests something else based in fear:

> whether primitive or not, mankind always stands on the brink of actions it performs itself but does not control (Jung, p. 25).

The psychologist is hinting at the unseen hand of the collective unconscious influencing us in ways beyond our comprehension. Elsewhere he makes this clearer:

> A wave of the unconscious may easily roll over [consciousness]... and then he forgets who he was and does things that are strange to him. Hence primitives are afraid of uncontrolled emotions... All man's strivings have therefore been directed towards the consolidation of consciousness. This was the purpose of rite and dogma; they were dams and walls to keep back the dangers of the unconscious. (ibid, p. 22)

Perhaps the false collective still plays the role of the dogma that Jung speaks of. His words suggest that the spooky depths of the unfathomable collective unconscious frighten us. Indeed, in chapter 11 of *The Bhagavad Gita*, the awesome and terrifying aspect of Brahman is revealed. Byung-Chul Han also captures some of these qualities in his description of true otherness. The true collective is not cuddly. It is not, as is the way of things in contemporary society, accessible, understandable, and familiar. In modern parlance we like to use the word *awesome* to describe neo-liberal objects and situations which are far from awesome. In true awe, however, there is an element which suggests terror and fear. Thankfully, the other face of awe is love. If one is afraid, and one sees the terror of the All more than one sees the love, then perhaps it is understandable that many turn away from Brahman, from the true collective and instead concern themselves with material, wherein there is an opportunity to dominate and control. One then need not feel fear, but sadly, will not experience a life lived in proximity to the stratosphere of love. Perhaps this is why societies have raised these elaborate false structures to distract themselves from the real. Perhaps it is not greed or lust, but fear; fear is the reason.

I am sat in *Moraira* café in Totley at the extreme south-western edge of Sheffield. A radio station is churning out popular music and I am listening in a detached manner. The news catches my attention. It is a timely and appropriate example of the way in which we have embedded the discourse of the false collective into our social structures. Why is it that in order to be granted a broadcast licence, a radio station is required to present news on the hour? News keeps us plugged into a narrative not necessarily of our choosing. The stories presented in those three-minute bulletins are not ones I would have chosen, were I able to do so. Furthermore, the headlines that were just forced upon me were closely related to others that I might hear or read in other media. Why is there this consensus about what is important? In sum, a synthetic reality is created, which society as a whole constructs and lives – in the current lexicon – rent free inside our heads. In this I am not considering metaphysics, only basic sociology – Noam Chomsky's 'five filters' for example. The false collective is a socio-psychological edifice – complex and intricate – which seemingly dominates our lives. The Vedantic sages of 300 BC, long before the advent of electronic technology, advised us to reject it and seek higher ends. I of course wholeheartedly concur, for if one spends enough time weighing the purpose of life, it soon becomes clear that acquiring wealth and power is ultimately futile. In common parlance we often say, 'you cannot take it with you'. I would respond 'take it where?'. In such figures of speech, we have a tacit acknowledgement of a greater or alternative reality, whether one is philosophically or spiritually inclined or not. The theorists mentioned throughout this text are of the same mind. Why obsess about the temporal, the fleeting? That beautiful body will age, the achievements of education, power and status will become historic footnotes and ultimately be forgotten. In sum (and the Vedantic texts and Sonya Richmond explain this far more powerfully than I can), a life well lived is one that is closer to the true collective. Loving those close to you *and* those who are random is the real path to ennoblement.

Black Music As Psychic Technology

One of the key themes of this essay is music. The oneness of Rastafarianism is closely aligned to reggae music, and the method and occasion that festivals offer for communing with the collective revolve around music performances. At various points in the text, I have referenced the idea that popular music has a particular power due to its origins as a technology developed by African victims of the transatlantic slave trade in order to help them to endure those four hundred years of horror. It is, I think, worth devoting a short chapter to this notion before I bring this volume to a close.

From the early twentieth century onwards, popular music has played a central role in the culture of western societies. Starting with the jazz age of the nineteen twenties, through the rock-and-roll phenomena in the post-war years, to grunge, hip-hop and rave in the nineteen nineties and beyond, music has defined the way that young people regard themselves as they mature into early adulthood and beyond. I hope that most readers are aware that most popular music forms are derived from the rhythms and styles of the African diaspora. I recognise of course that early on, the African core of the original forms was embellished using, and also later overlaid with, folk and similar genres. Nevertheless, the originality and spirit at the heart of the new musical genres was African.

That early Afro-diasporic forms were also a reaction to slavery and oppression is well documented. Slavery placed limits on African property ownership and literacy. Oral music traditions were one of the few aspects of the slaves' lives that they could be said to own. No doubt this facet is important; it is what gave the music its power. Music became one of the few resources which they could use to transcend the horror which surrounded them. They were therefore motivated and able to carefully develop this facility. Some even label the music of that period as a "superpower", although for purely material reasons. Examples given include the idea that secret messages could be encoded in songs to facilitate the exchange of illicit information. The emotional content of music was also useful to help convince others of the case for emancipation. However, I prefer to label the music of this period a *psychic technology* because it may have been the means by which the Afro-diasporic performers and audiences were able to connect to the collective unconscious. This perhaps, was the manner in which music helped them to escape the acute anguish of their bondage. Many of the features of the early genres – spiritualism, call and response, work songs, field hollers – were to my ears, collective incantations for this purpose.

Nevertheless, to describe the origins of black music in this way – that is, as simply a resource to help African slaves to deal with the overwhelming negativity that surrounded them, neglects a crucial detail. It is necessary, I think, to attribute emancipation as an equally important factor in the development of the psychic technology of this artform. The freeing of the slaves was perhaps the big bang event which injected optimism into the already powerful survival forms. In 1865 (in the USA), the singular event of liberation infused the cannon with positive elements which increased its relevance to those who were not shackled in misery, who were actually *enjoying* their material existence. In other words, white society. Now happier songs – about a boy, or about a girl, or about future hopes and desires – could also make use of the powerful language originally created for survival and turn it into a method for expressing yearning and happiness.

The misery of enslavement and oppression, allied to the joy and hope of emancipation may then have been the unique elements which created the twentieth century incarnations of black music (and is why those who argue that 'rock-and-roll was created by Bill Haley and The Comets' are missing a stack load of crucial explanatory details). The undeniable double-barrelled potency of the new psychic technology, birthed via the very specific horror-circumstances of its origins, powered an unstoppable sweep across the world. From the United States to Berlin and Paris. To England, Scandinavia, Japan, and Russia. The subsequent and continual interplay between the American forms, and other black idioms from Africa, South America, and the Caribbean continued the development of the music. No comparable entertainment had ever been experienced. Black music was irresistible.

It could even be argued that the popular creative output of America in the twentieth century smoothed the transition of the USA from large colonial outpost to the Pax Americana superpower. Jazz is claimed to be the only original American artform, and as Joel Dinerstein argued in *The Origins of Cool in Postwar America*, the idea of cool as exemplified by Brando, Dean, Bogart, and Sinatra arose from jazz music and its associated communities. Indeed, that mid-twentieth-century language: 'dough', 'bread', 'hipster' –

and even the modern usage of the word 'cool' itself – originated in African -American culture. This is to say nothing of the popular music made by white musicians. Bing Crosby and Frank Sinatra, through Elvis Presley, Bill Haley, The Beatles, The Rolling Stones, David Bowie, Sting and Joe Strummer have all made explicit their debt to, or affinity with, black music. Therefore, some, or perhaps much of the soft power that America enjoyed in the last century derived from its popular art, which in turn either directly originated from, or owed a huge debt to black music and culture. This wasn't acknowledged of course. Attempts have frequently been made to even obscure the origins of popular music. For example, consider the hip-hop track *Jazz Thing* by Gang Starr which is a quite remarkable potted history of jazz in verse. The rapper Guru barks out the following stanza:

> Now listen see
> The real mystery is a music history
> Created by Whiteman or any other white man
> That pretended he originated
> And contended that he innovated
> A jazz thing.

The lyric makes reference to one Paul Whiteman, the so-called 'King of Jazz' who was voted 'entertainer of the year' by Variety magazine in 1922. Whiteman was a Caucasian male; Guru is highlighting the mendacious attempts to purloin this music, the one thing that the African diaspora in the USA was able to own and develop, from its true creators.

In Joel Dinerstein's *Jazz: A quick immersion*, the author attempted to describe what the black jazz musicians were striving to achieve artistically, and to some extent, psychologically, in the early twentieth century. He cites Mezz Mezzrow, a Jewish-American clarinettist who in nineteen forty-six wrote:

> the colored people, fresh up out of three hundred years of slavery, still the despised pariahs of the country in spite of their 'liberation'... had roared out a revolutionary new music to shout [a] message to the world" (Dinerstein, 2020).

What is this message that Dinerstein and Mezzrow detected in these forms? It relates to something other than a materialist sociology, which is why I chose to employ the label *psychic technology*. The secret payload of jazz, and perhaps that which lies behind the popularity of the entire Afro-diasporic cannon, is a message which encourages listeners to live in a different way to that expected by society. It is implicitly a message of freedom, immaterialism, and non-conformism, which is why it has always appealed to the young. Unlike European technologies, it is not rooted in physicalist assumptions; it is to be lived and felt. Its methodology is a social and experiential one; it involves listening, copying, and embellishing; call and response. Malcolm James' 2021 volume, *Sonic Impact* analyses the more recent black music genres of reggae, jungle, and grime. James describes contemporary socio-psychological processes which resemble the operation of the earlier forms. It is possible then, that not only were psychic technologies present in nineteenth and early twentieth-century black music, but James also finds equivalents in their electronic and information age descendants.

In the essay *The Meaning and Destiny of Western Culture*, Bernardo Kastrup muses upon the functions of logic and reason espoused by the ancient Greek philosopher Parmenides, and which are the basis of western philosophy and science. Kastrup invokes Peter Kingsley's argument that the west may have misinterpreted Parmenides. Kingsley suggested that the Greek thinker's intention was not to demand that logic be applied as a set of rules, rather it should be an *incantation* to aid the breaking down of the material illusion and attempt to access the truer reality behind it. If material reality is an illusion, one that is sticky and pervasive, then according to this argument, Parmenides saw the need for a persuasive cognitive technology to dismantle it. Kastrup suggests that according to Kingsley, logic played this role. This brief essay was an epiphany.

Following Kingsley's lead, I feel able to posit that the entire cannon of black music has been an effort to achieve that which Parmenides sought. The occasions and methods are completely different; not via the 'incantation' of logic in the academies, but rather through a collective participation in rhythm and melody has the African diaspora sought to shatter the material illusion. In the conceptual language of Kingsley, blues is incantation, as is jazz, funk, and soul. The method was something akin to the following. Firstly, a leadership role is assigned to the musically gifted in the community. They are tasked with creating the sounds and in this respect, leading the group effort. The other people in the space are required to fully participate as listener or dancer. Note that this contribution is equal in value to that of the musicians. Assembled thus, the black community are able to incant collectively, and the group meditation would eventually bring them to an understanding of a different reality. Music is used in Afro-diasporic cultures as the occasion for a group swim in the pool of the collective unconscious. Viewed from the negative perspective, this process transports the participants beyond the troublesome material domain, at least temporarily. From the positive point of view, it takes them higher.

In 1970, the band Funkadelic scored an underground hit with the record *Free Your Mind and Your Ass Will Follow*. The 'free your mind' aspect of the title is an exhortation to escape from the bonds of the illusion of material reality. In Vedantic philosophy, there exists the comparable notion of *Maya* or illusion which is to be transcended if one is to achieve *moksha* or liberation. However, in respect of the premise of black music as a psychic technology, reversing the clauses in the song title might make a more powerful statement. That is, once we free our asses (on the dancefloor via good music), there is a possibility that our minds might also be released from the material illusion and then be able to commune with the collective consciousness. Interaction with this alternative reality or mind, is perhaps, the true goal of black music.

An unintended consequence of black psychic technology might be that it tends to present a challenge to established power structures in society. For instance, in the past, slaves and their descendants were unable to confront authority directly. However, the creation of these musical forms allowed the displaced Africans to not only cock a very oblique snook at the powerful, but also – over the course of the twentieth century – to subtly undermine the old methods of maintaining hegemony. This occurred without the awareness of the authorities; after all, what could be more innocuous than musical entertainment? As stated at the start of this section, the slave societies which had created this music, were allowed very little in terms of material consolations. Therefore, their technologies sought to leapfrog the quotidian and reach towards the collective strata of existence that modern philosophies such as analytic idealism describe. Perhaps it was the only way of surviving so complete a subjugation as the transatlantic slave trade. However, and this is the point, as a technology of the collective, it inadvertently communicated to those beyond the immediate black communities – to poor, freedom seeking, and open-minded people. This music ushered in a revolution of sorts! The changed attitudes and rebelliousness of pop-music-loving teenagers in the twentieth century was evidence of that fact.

On reflection, perhaps the authorities were not completely blind to the danger. Slave owners appeared to exhibit an unnatural fear of the drum. 'Drums were banned to slaves in every Southern state but Louisiana. [...] Georgia banned "all drums, horns or other loud instruments which may give sign or notice of wicked designs or intentions"' (Dinerstein 2020; p29). The Louisiana exception is cited as the reason that jazz originated in the city of New Orleans. There were similar restrictions in some Caribbean states which led, for example, to the innovation of the steel drum to circumnavigate the ban on percussive instruments. Were slave owners implicitly cognisant of a black philosophy of sound, radically different to European materialist philosophies? Did they somehow sense a technology of the collective unconscious? Due to the fact that materialist thinking was *de rigueur* in European society, it would not have been possible to air these suspicions explicitly. Hence, perhaps, the prohibitions were based upon rationales that were highly dubious.

Therefore, it might be possible that with this music, black communities were not contesting their oppressors in the material domain, rather their music was challenging materialist might in another plane of reality altogether. Open-minded others who heard the music unconsciously understood the other-worldly message, but the ingrained materialism of western philosophy blind-sided those who wielded power in society. It nearly worked. When in the nineteen fifties and nineteen sixties young westerners, swayed by the appeal of (Afro-diasporic) rock and roll challenged the rather staid conventions that their elders had expected them to follow, mainstream America was outraged. In the 1990s rave culture, rap, and grunge utterly seduced swathes of both black and white young people. This situation was considered problematic for the status quo and the authorities responded. In the UK the 1994 *Criminal Justice and Public Order Act* was enacted. Part V of the act included sections to restrict raves, for example, outlawing certain types of 'repetitive beats' in particular contexts. This is reminiscent of the outlawing of the drum in previous times.

If we accept that black music forms are offensive technologies in the fight against a materialistic mode of existence, then neo-liberal capitalism is the countermeasure of the avaricious class to it. It may be true that black music technologies of consciousness scored victories in the twentieth century, however, at the current time neo-liberal capitalism has roared back with a vengeance. If we are to heap praise on the black music pioneers for the creation of such a stealthily powerful idiom, then we also need to admire neo-liberal capitalists for the manner in which they completely reversed the discourse of freedom. Black music avowed freedom as a pathway to an ineffable collective. Neo-liberal capitalism now does not deny the importance of freedom, but rather it has altered its meaning. In a mendacious twist, it redefined freedom from being a tool for breaking down materialism, to a means to wallow in the pervasive illusion itself. Neo-liberal freedom is freedom to enslave oneself in materialism via consumption. Western society promotes this message at every turn and the distracted citizen is easily suckered.

As Han suggested, neo-liberal capitalism tends to devour all that it comes in contact with, including that most precious to a society. It will purloin anything – the profane, the sacred and all that is in between – and seek to fashion it for its own purposes. It is for this reason that creative valuables or cherished psychological processes should be kept out of sight when neo-liberal capitalism is in the room. Its telos is utterly materialistic – the sole valued outcome is profit. At the current time, having co-opted powerful digital technologies in its service, it has locked in its recent gains. It controls many of the means of creative dissemination with the result that valuable work is difficult to obscure from the machine. At this point, black psychic technologies appear rather primitive and defeated. However, in previous centuries the same might have been said when comparing muskets, cannons, and warships to African drums. Technology of the ephemeral is very difficult to pin down, let alone outflank.

This then, is our hope and perhaps our template. The African slaves found themselves in a so-called new world where the most advanced material technologies were employed to keep them in bondage. Their only recourse was to reach for the collective. This provided them with strength and fortitude and most importantly, a means of escape. While it didn't free them materially, it was a freedom of the psyche; an implicit rebellion which continued to challenge materialism long after emancipation. One could form loose parallels between the historical bondage of the African diaspora and the present serfdom of the digital era – although the suffering of the latter epoch is not in the same cosmos as the former. Nevertheless, perhaps the psychic technologies bequeathed to us by those black communities might be useful in our modern-day struggles. Moreover, can we learn from what they did and create our own twenty-first century psychologies to help us resist the digital onslaught? Remember, the cage door is already open. The key – or the weapon, if you prefer a military metaphor – is your mind and your soul. Use them wisely – and be free.

Deus and Coltrane

I have nearly reached the end of my Moleskine notebook and feel that I have said all that I have to say. At this moment, I am feeling a little like John Coltrane, the renowned jazz saxophonist. Indeed, Coltrane is an artist who exemplifies the Afro-diasporic yearning for the collective unconscious through music. However, this is not my point. I am referring to the reported recording session in which Coltrane was playing one of his elaborate and extremely long solos. When he had finished, he felt that he needed to apologise to the band leader, Miles Davis, for taking up too much time in the particular number. 'I just don't know how to stop' protested Coltrane. Davis, razor-sharp as always replied, 'It's easy. Just take the horn out of your [expletive] mouth'.

Thus, the time has come for me to quit blowing. I will leave you with a question. Is the transpersonal mentation, the collective unconscious and Brahman equivalent to the human notion of God? Many scholars of Vedantic thought would answer in the affirmative with regards to Brahman because the ancient Indian texts are regarded as both philosophical and theological. Furthermore, any reading of Sheldrake in, for example, *Ways to Go Beyond*, will reveal support for this idea from the molecular biologist also. The last word will go to Carl Gustav Jung. It is taken from a jewel of a BBC television interview recorded in March 1959, when the psychologist was eighty-three years old. Interviewer John Freeman posed questions related to the early life of the old professor:

Freeman: Did [your father] make you attend church regularly?

Jung: Oh that was quite natural. Everybody went to church on Sunday.

Freeman: And did you believe in God?

Jung: Oh yes.

Freeman: Do you *now* believe in God?

Jung: Now? [*Pauses*]

Jung: Difficult to answer [*Pauses*]

Jung: I know [*Smiles*]

Jung: I don't need to believe. I know.

References

Chalmers, David. 1995. Facing up to the problem of consciousness, *Journal of Consciousness Studies*. 1(3): 200-219.

Csikszentmihalyi, Mihaly & Judith LeFevre. 1989. Optimal experiences in work and leisure. *Journal of Personality and Social Psychology*, 56, 815-822.

Coldewey, Devin. 2022. "Space Billboards Could Cost $65m and Still Turn a Profit". *Tech Crunch*. Available at: https://techcrunch.com/2022/10/05/ space-billboards-could-cost-65m-and-still-turn-a-profit (Accessed 5 October 2023).

Dahl, Roald. 1979. "The Wonderful Story of Henry Sugar" *The Wonderful Story of Henry Sugar and Six More*. London: Penguin.

Debord, Guy. 1983. *Society of the Spectacle*. Detroit: Black & Red.

Dinerstein, Joel. 2017. *The Origins of Cool in Postwar America*. University of Chicago Press.

Dinerstein Joel. 2020. *Jazz. A Quick Immersion*. New York: Tibidabo.

Diski, Jenny. 2009. *Skating To Antarctica*. London: Profile Books.

Face to Face – Carl Gustav Jung. 1959. TV Broadcast. UK: BBC. Available at: https://www.bbc.co.uk/iplayer/episode/p04qhvyj/face-to-face-carl-jung (Accessed 5 October 2023).

Fela Kuti – Interview 1988 (Reeling In The Years Archive). 1988. YouTube Video. Available at: https://youtu.be/QtiAnjtYdwo. (Accessed 5 October 2023).

Flynn, Thomas. 2006. *Existentialism: A Very Short Introduction*. Oxford University Press.

Fuller, Steve. 2023. "The Scientific Revolution as Augustinian Modernism" *YouTube*. Available at: https://youtu.be/J7CmpSITySc (Accessed 11 November 2023).

Gang Starr. 1990. "Jazz Thing" Track 8 on Music From Mo' Better Blues. CBS, CD.

Han, Byung-Chul. 2018. *The Expulsion of the Other*. Cambridge: Polity.

James, Malcolm. 2020. *Sonic Intimacy*. New York: Bloomsbury.

Jung, Carl Gustav. 2014. *The Archetypes and the Collective Unconscious*. London: Routledge.

Vasquez, Kuauhtli. 2020. "Universal Consciousness". *YouTube*. Available at: https://youtu.be/u3-nPeFgcvM (Accessed 26 June 2024).

Kastrup, Bernardo. 2014. *Why Materialism Is Baloney: How true skeptics know there is no death and fathom answers to life, the universe, and everything*. Winchester, UK: IFF.

Kastrup, Bernardo. 2020. *Science Ideated*. Winchester, UK: IFF.

Kern, Leslie. 2022. *Gentrification Is Inevitable and Other Lies*. London: Verso.

Kuhn, Thomas. 1962. *The Structure of Scientific Revolutions*. University of Chicago Press.

Lachman, Gary. 2020. *Dreaming Ahead of Time*. Edinburgh: Floris.

Lanier, Jaron. 2010. *You Are Not a Gadget*. New York: Knopf.

Lawson, Hilary. 2001. *Closure: A Story of Everything*. London: Routledge

Markoff, John. 2005. *What The Dormouse Said. How the sixties counter-culture shaped the personal computer industry*. New York: Penguin.

Markus, Hazel & Keith Sentis. 1982. The self in social information processing. In J. Suls (ed.) *Psychological Perspectives on the Self (Vol. 1)* New Jersey: Earlbaum.

Mascaró, Juan. 1962. *The Bhagavad Gita*. London: Penguin.

Mascaró, Juan. 1965. *The Upanishads*. London: Penguin.

McLuhan, Herbert Marshall & Quentin Fiore. 1967. *The Medium is the Massage*. London: Penguin.

Money Bots. 2020. TV Documentary. Directed by Friedrich Moser and Daniel Andrew Wunderer. France: Arte.

Moody, Raymond A. 2001. *Life After Life*. Random House.

Nagel, Ralph. 2014. *Mind and Cosmos*. Oxford University Press.

Parnia, Sam. 2014. Death and consciousness—an overview of the mental and cognitive experience of death. *Annals of the New York Academy of Sciences* 1330 (1): 75-93.

Polinghorne, John. 2002. *Quantum Theory: A Very Short Introduction*. Oxford University Press.

Richmond, Sonya. 1971. *Common Sense About Yoga*. London: MacGibbon & Kee.

Rousseau, Jean-Jacques. 1993. *Émile* (B. Foxley, Trans.). London: J. M. Dent. (Original work published in 1762).

Sheckley, Robert. 1975. "Specialist" *The Robert Sheckley Omnibus*. London: Penguin.

Sheldrake, Rupert. 1992. An experimental test of the hypothesis of formative causation. *Rivista di Biologia - Biology Forum* 86: 431-444.

Sheldrake, Rupert. 2003. The sense of being stared at: Part 1: Is it real or illusory? *Journal of Consciousness Studies* 12: 32-49.

Sheldrake, Rupert. 2011. *The Presence of the Past: Morphic resonance and the habits of nature*. London: Icon.

Sheldrake, Rupert. 2019. *Ways To Go Beyond And Why They Work: Spiritual practices in a scientific age*. London: Coronet.

Sheldrake, Rupert & Pamela Smart. 1998. A dog that seems to know when its owner is returning: preliminary investigations. *Journal of the Society for Psychical Research*, 62, 220-232.

Sumner, Seirian. 2022. *Endless Forms*. London: Collins.

The Century of the Self. 2002, TV Documentary. Directed by Adam Curtis. UK: BBC. Available at: https://www.bbc.co.uk/programmes/p00ghx6g (Accessed 11 November 2023).

The World Cup: A Captain's Tale. 1982. TV Drama. Directed by Tom Clegg. UK: Tyne Tees Television.

Tucker, Jim. 2008.Children's Reports of Past-Life Memories: A Review, *Explore* 4, (4): 244-248.

Van Lommel, Pim & Ruud van Wees & Vincent Meyers & Ingrid Elfferich. 2001. Near-death experience in survivors of cardiac arrest: a prospective study in the Netherlands. *The Lancet 358*.

Waking Life. 1999. DVD. Directed by Richard Linklater. USA: 20th Century Fox.

Acknowledgements

There are many who aside from the author, bear responsibility for this book. I could go back as far as my infancy in the list of those who have inspired or helped to develop my ability to form ideas such as these. However, for the sake of brevity I shall mainly restrict myself to those whose sphere of influence has been more recent.

I would firstly like to thank everyone involved with a magical tent which appears every summer in a corner of the WOMAD UK festival site. Specifically, I would like to acknowledge the regular DJs: Mark Keshishian, Steve and Adam Isbell (the Racubah brothers), Ebou Touray and Nicola Sokell. Also included in the above is Martin Daws, a poet who in that space adopts the important Afro-diasporic persona of the M.C., the role of which is to encourage dancers to reach for the collective. I extend additional thanks to Jim Cousins who runs the operation and to Jess, one of the team members. It was a conversation with the latter at six a.m., at the end of a great night in 2023 which inspired me to knuckle down to complete this volume. Over the years, my experiences in that venue, in the deep, late hours of night have helped me to achieve greater insight into the nature of things.

In addition to the above, I also thank my wife Dee who creates a peaceful home environment in which it is possible to ponder weighty concepts. We have also shared numerous 'Sheldrakian moments' which are always a direct challenge to the materialism that society demands we accept. I would like to acknowledge Jason Fletcher who read an early draft of this text and his enthusiasm for the ideas within provided the motivation I needed during the arduous editing process. Lastly, a shout out to Holly Fairbrother who introduced me to Byung-Chul Han and whose intense philosophical questioning over a period of around two years helped me to adopt a firm position on various topics.

Thanks are further extended to Hilary Lawson, founder of the *How The Light Gets In* philosophy and music festival held every May in Hay-On-Wye. This festival has provided an amateur philosopher such as myself with access to ideas and thinkers including Mary Midgley, Gary Lachman, Bernardo Kastrup, Steve Fuller, and Joel Dinerstein. I probably would not have discovered the work of these great minds without the efforts of Lawson and his team.

Retreating further back in time, I wish to express my love for the members of my original nuclear family: my parents who encouraged me to commune with the light rather than darkness, my eldest brother who nurtured my passion for black music, my other older brother who has always inspired me to be creative. The family of my youngest brother has provided insights into the native wisdom of young people, and this gives me hope for the future. I feel that these acknowledgements would be incomplete without two further references. Firstly, to the nineteen eighties sound systems of North-West London with whom I served my musical apprenticeship: *Romancer*, *King Majesty*, *Quattro* and *Emotions*. Secondly, to my friends and colleagues during my undergraduate years at the University of Sussex in the nineteen nineties who, in many different ways, encouraged my intellectualism and open-mindedness to flourish.

I write most effectively in cafés. Therefore, please allow me to convey my appreciation to those establishments which offered inspiring environments during the summer of 2023. They include *Kollective Kitchen* in Nether Edge, Sheffield; *Les Delices d'Arianne* in Lattes, Herault, France; *S17* in Bradway, Sheffield and *Barista Club* in Bilbao, Spain.

Finally, to the randomers. To you, the other members of the collective with whom I have no material relations. In other words, people with whom I have shared smiles, hugs, and conversations everywhere, but especially at festivals and night spots. In particular, the dancers. For me, the most profound method of experiencing the wonder of the collective is through dancing in a room full of strangers, individuals yet unified, breaking down boundaries and pushing love through the golden thread which connects us.

I am grateful to you all.

About Callum Bell

Callum Bell was born in London in the 1960s. His parents arrived in the United Kingdom in the 1950s having emigrated from the Caribbean island of Grenada.

He has two degrees in psychology: a BA from the University of Sussex and an MSc from the University of Sheffield. His other academic interests include philosophy and sociology.

He has a passion for music of all genres. This has manifested itself in time spent as an extra-curricular rapper and sound system MC in the nineteen eighties, a DJ in the nineteen nineties and noughties, and a guitarist/songwriter throughout his adult life. He also writes poetry. And dances.

Callum has spent many years working in the technology industry, spanning a period that begins when micro computers were obscure playthings for nerds, to today's digitally addicted society.

He currently lives in Sheffield, South Yorkshire.